The Lizard Man Speaks

Number Twenty-six
THE CORRIE HERRING HOOKS SERIES

Eric R. Pianka

THE LIZARD MAN SPEAKS

UNIVERSITY OF TEXAS PRESS
Austin

Requests for permission to reproduce material from this work
should be sent to Permissions, University of Texas Press,
Box 7819, Austin, TX 78713-7819.

⊚ The paper used in this publication meets the minimum requirements
of American National Standard for Information Sciences—Permanence
of Paper for Printed Library Materials, ANSI Z39.48-1984.

LIBRARY OF CONGRESS CATALOGING-IN-PUBLICATION DATA

Pianka, Eric R.
    The lizard man speaks / Eric R. Pianka. — 1st ed.
        p.   cm. — (The Corrie Herring Hooks series ; no. 26)
    Includes bibliographic references (p.   ) and index.
    ISBN 0-292-76552-5 (cloth)
      1. Pianka, Eric R. 2. Zoologists — United States — Biography.
    3. Lizards. I. Title. II. Series.
    QL31.P57A3   1994
    597.95'092—dc20
    [B]   93-38067

To a tough and sometimes dirty dozen
my field assistants

CONTENTS

PREFACE

THIS IS A REAL-LIFE ADVENTURE BOOK, STORIES ABOUT LIVING in remote wilderness areas studying wild lizards in their natural habitats. I have lived four full years of my adult life in the Australian outback, often alone. I can be comfortable without human companionship for extended periods of time, something that most of my friends cannot fathom. (Indeed, most of them say it would drive them crazy!) A wise fellow hermit once said, "Occasionally I read a newspaper or listen to the radio to find out what my fellow humans are doing, but I'll be damned if I will track them down in their natural habitat [cities]!"

What could have prompted such a self-imposed exile from civilization and humanity? What was this really all about? I work in the Australian outback to collect scientific data and to try to expand our understanding of natural ecological systems. The time and space scale over which the fire succession cycle occurs is vast and could not be studied anywhere except in central Australia. But this was also a sort of religious pilgrimage for me, a return to nature. I perceive some input from our primitive hunter-gatherer instincts. I am exceedingly fortunate to be a field biologist, and I am privileged to have had the many experiences recounted here—even most of the hardships have been enjoyable in their own memorable way.

In the end, the question may not be so much Why did I write this little book? but rather Why did you read it? I long for a simpler existence. I despise standing in lines or waiting for traffic lights to change. Objects and noises of human origin are obnoxious to me. I hate being fenced in, unable even to get off the road. I cannot tolerate the thought of a world in which I can't get to pristine wilderness, let alone a world without any wilderness at all. (We seem to be almost impervious to, and unaware of, changes occurring around us, perhaps because they occur on a time scale of decades, too slow to be perceived. But, if one could travel from the 1960s to the 1990s, the response might be more like "Hey, wait a minute!" Unfortunately, much of the younger generation doesn't even know what they've lost, and are losing.) We don't improve on nature as we landscape and pave over the surface of the planet. I think buildings, fences, and roads are ugly. I keep coming back to the outback in yet another futile attempt to escape from creations of human origin, crowding, overpopulation, and regimentation. My ex-wife Helen used to say that I was born a century too late. Perhaps we all were. Perhaps you read this in your own attempt to escape from urbanization.

The Lizard Man Speaks

Beginnings

Just as any American is a "gringo" to a Mexican, any American is a "Yank" to an Australian. Any Brit is a "pommie" or a "pom." Aussies have little or no appreciation for the subtlety of northerners versus southerners, let alone the Mason-Dixon line. Most Australians seem predisposed to like Yanks and poms, although occasionally one detects some resentment that we exert hidden controls on their lives. This seems rather peculiar to me, since I perceive Australia to be racing as fast as it can to become another U. S. of A. Indeed, of the two dozen countries I have visited, Australia, Canada, and the United States not only are the most similar but also offer by far the most freedom and the finest quality of life.

People are distributed unevenly across Australia: 99 percent of them live on only 1 percent of the surface, packed in like sardines and stacked up like cordwood. The other 99 percent of Australia is wide open space, containing a mere 1 percent of the population. Almost everybody lives in and around only a handful of cities: Adelaide, Brisbane, Canberra, Darwin, Melbourne, Perth, or Sydney. Smaller cities, such as Alice Springs, Broken Hill, and Kalgoorlie, support modest populations. The vast area of uninhabitable inland generates extremely low continent-wide population density statistics, but Australia is far from being underpopulated. Habitable places are more than saturated with people. The prime land is all taken. Australia already has more than enough mouths to feed. I'm acutely aware of the importance of cities as essential support systems for specialized goods and services, but, alas, I am no city slicker—this Yank spends his time down under in the bush.

Once, on a long cab ride from Toronto along the north shore of Lake Ontario, I found myself discussing the Canadian wilds with the cab driver. I was dumbfounded when he referred to them as "wasteland." I tried, probably unsuccessfully, to convince him that uninhabited Canada had immense value as a pristine area representing natural habitat, even though it wasn't yet being extensively exploited by humans. Wilderness areas, unspoiled by human hands, constitute a real but vanishing treasure. When was the last time you were all alone, miles from anyone else, warmed by a campfire out under the stars? If you have never enjoyed such an experience, you should do it soon, for the very opportunity is rapidly disappearing. When you first arrive in a wilderness from the hustle and bustle of civilization with which we are all too familiar, the silence is always a jolt. At first, you feel as if you must be going deaf—there are no noises of human origin whatsoever. Your sense of hearing seems to become more acute after a time, making it difficult to readjust to the noises of "civilization" upon your return to it.

I'm in one of the last such terrestrial frontiers now, at latitude 28°12' S by longitude 123°35' E in the uninhabited Great Victoria Desert in central Western Australia at my favorite place on this planet, a magnificent study site I call "Red Sands." Most people think of deserts as barren, lifeless places. Nothing could be further from the truth—most deserts are teeming with life.

The only sound one hears out here almost continuously is the desert wind, which is often fierce. In the summer, it blows like a blast furnace, desiccating everything before it relentlessly. In the winter, ruthless antarctic icy cold winds stream in from the south. Strong continuous winds sometimes get on your nerves. Listen carefully, for soft winds generate a multitude of sounds: a light breeze produces a lullaby, a delicate rustling of the *Acacia* needles on a nearby mulga tree; one can hear a willy willy (an Aussie term for a whirlwind) coming from a long way off; I have heard a strong front roaring in from afar like a freight train for what seemed to be half a minute before it hit! Another rare but welcome sound is thunder, heralding rain. Other natural noises, such as the birds and crickets singing, abound at times. At night, the distinctive calls of Frogmouths, Mopokes, and Boobook Owls can often be heard in the distance. Occasionally, you hear the deep wheezing bellow of a bull camel herding his harem along. In the morning and evening, pairs of beautiful pink-and-gray Galah Cockatoos fly over in formation, squawking shrilly. Flocks of Green Budgerigars (parakeets) sometimes fly by, chattering. The Crested Bellbird sings its song in morse code: dit, dit, . . . dah, dah, dit. By far the most melodious and pleasant bird song in the Great Victoria Desert is that of the Pied Butcherbird, a large black-and-white, vaguely shrikelike bird. Its repertoire is very varied, like that of an American mockingbird, but louder. Butcherbirds sing especially vociferously about dawn and dusk, advertising their presence to other butcherbirds. I always get a kick out of whistling an imitation of a variant of their song that I call "Where have my people gone? My people will return!" (referring to the vanished Aborigines).

Where have my peo-ple   gone?   My peo-ple will   re-turn!

When I do this for the first time, nearby birds sometimes respond by answering loudly—other birds fly away surreptitiously as if outsung! I suspect that the former are older birds confident of their territorial boundaries, whereas the latter are younger birds insecure about territorial disputes.

This particular site supports a higher biodiversity of lizards than anywhere else in the entire world, a phenomenal forty-seven different species of lizards in five families. These include huge perenties (aptly named *Varanus giganteus* by scientists), a full two meters in total length, magnificent relatives of the awesome Komodo dragons of the Lesser Sunda Islands of Indonesia. Monitor lizards are known as "goannas" in Australia. (This is probably a corruption of "iguana," although varanids are not at all close to iguanines—indeed, among lizards they may well be closest to snakes!) Several related varanid species, known as pygmy monitors, are smaller but equally stunning. There are dozens of species of skinks here and almost as many geckos, exquisitely beautiful nocturnal lizards. Nearly legless snakelike pygopodids (sometimes termed "flap-footed" lizards) plus a host of agamid lizards are also present. One of the latter that is particularly spectacular is the so-called thorny devil (sometimes referred to as a "mountain devil"—its scientific name[1] is *Moloch horridus*). These spiny agamids are reminiscent, both anatomically and ecologically, of distantly related American horned lizards. In short, Australia is a biological wonderland. For a biologist, being here is much better than being turned loose in a gigantic outdoor zoo.

Why are the Australian deserts so rich in species of lizards? The challenge of explaining this high diversity and of understanding what goes on between component species is awesome. Compared with Australian deserts, North American deserts are quite impoverished, with only a dozen species of lizards; in the Kalahari semidesert of southern Africa, only twenty species occur. How do so many lizards avoid competition and manage to coexist? How do they partition resources such as food and microhabitats? Ecologists still know surprisingly little about exactly how diverse natural ecological systems function—ecological understanding that is much needed and that will be critical to our own survival as well as that of other species of animals and plants. In fact, the Australian deserts probably offer the last opportunity to study the regional effects of disturbance on local diversity (see Chapter 8).

Sands in the Australian desert are rich in iron and are therefore usually a delicate pale rusty red, almost flesh color. Long undulating sandridges provide attractive curves to create a sensuous image of Mother Earth. Equally curvaceous, evergreen marble gum trees (*Eucalyptus gongylocarpa*) with their smooth white bark adorn this splendid landscape. There are no cactus here, although prickly pear has been introduced in eastern Australia. The dominant plant is porcupine grass, *Triodia basedowi*, often called "spinifex," which grows in unique hummock tussocks unlike grasses anywhere else in the world. This is Crown land (owned by the Australian government), an exceedingly attractive, semipristine place. Early on, each time I left, I thought that I'd never return. But now I know better. I can't seem to get Australia out of my system; I keep coming back here, again and again. My first trip down under was a quarter of a century ago in 1966. I've been back several times since then and have lived nearly four full years in the outback.

It is January 1991. I have been at this remote study area for almost two weeks and haven't seen another human for nearly that long. I treasure my solitude, space, privacy, peace, and tranquility. I'm a desert rat in my element. Deserts are clean, unspoiled places with magnificent vistas plus rich floras and faunas. This tale has no real beginning and certainly no end (at least not until I die), so I will begin

by taking a chronological path. My intent is certainly not to give you an autobiography (to my mind, these should be posthumous); but rather I want to try to provide some historical background, to give some insight into my past and perhaps myself.

When I was about six years old in the mid-1940s, soon after the end of the Second World War, my parents drove our family east from our hometown, Yreka, near Oregon in far northern California. We went across the United States to visit our paternal grandparents, German immigrants who lived in Illinois. Somewhere along the way in the South, we stopped at a roadside park for a picnic lunch. There I saw my first lizard, a gorgeous, green, sleek, long-tailed arboreal creature (later I determined that this must have been an *Anolis carolinensis*) climbing around in some vines. We did our utmost to capture that lizard, but all we were able to get was its tail. I still remember standing there holding its twitching tail, wishing intensely that it was the lizard instead. About a year later back in California, I caught my first garter snake, which I tried to keep as a "pet," however, it soon escaped (snakes aren't pets, but they are escape artists!). In the third grade, I discovered that the classroom next door had a captive

ABOVE LEFT:
Parents, Gini and Walt, at cabin in winter in the Greenhorn mountains above Yreka where Eric was conceived (1938)

ABOVE RIGHT:
Two-year-old Ricky with his father, Walt (Hilt, California, 1941)

Brothers Rick and Mike Pianka play in a field (Yreka, August, 1946).

baby alligator. I was transfixed by that alligator and stood by its aquarium for hours on end reveling in its every move. As a little boy, I was destined to become a biologist, long before I had any inkling about what science was. Years later, in graduate school, I discovered the layers in the biological cake, and eventually I went on to earn a Ph.D., and, later, my D. Sc. as an ecologist.

My hometown, Yreka, the seat of Siskiyou County in the shadow of Mount Shasta, was a sleepy little town of about 3,500 people in those days, surrounded by relatively pristine wilderness. My boyhood was rich, replete with the great outdoors and lots of adventure. It was an easy walk out our back door to a variety of relatively undisturbed natural habitats. After school, my brother Mike and I roamed the juniper-covered hills around town catching snakes and lizards. We lived outside and knew virtually every hectare within several miles of town. I collected everything from rocks to insects (especially butter-flies) to bird eggs to lizards and snakes, including rattlesnakes. My collections were semiprofessional, too, with every specimen dutifully labeled with its scientific name. I went to great trouble to build a glass display case to house my collection of bird eggs, and we went to even greater lengths to find the nests of all the local species, ranging from hummingbirds to great horned owls. I kept the snakes and lizards alive, and when they died, dutifully pickled them in denatured alcohol as proper museum specimens.

In the early 1950s, we began to play serious war games with rubber guns and opposing teams: if you were hit, you were out of the game for the remainder of that day. We dug foxholes and trenches and even hidden tunnels in our main "battlefield," several large open lots behind our house. One of our favorite places to play was Yreka Creek, which also held its share of neat animals. I recall once creeping stealthily down a trail in dense vegetation leading my small band "on patrol," and hearing our "enemies" coming the other way. At my silent signal, we dove into the bushes alongside the trail, only to discover that we were in a patch of nettles! But we had the fortitude to lie there unflinching for long seconds until the "enemy" came around the corner into full view. We ambushed them, taking them totally by surprise and splaying them with stout rubber bands. We "won" the battle that day, although we paid for our victory with welts all over our bodies.

I became a Boy Scout and was looking forward to going on a two-week-long scout summer camping expedition in the wild along Beaver Creek, a tributary of the untamed Klamath River. Walking back from a scout meeting with a friend one night in early April of 1952, we were amazed and excited to see what appeared to be a fireworks display off in the distance south of town. Bright arcs of light shot through the air, punctuated with explosions and bursts and flashes of light. We raced home only to discover that it was too late for us to go, but that my brother Mike had gone to watch the National Guardsmen display their military equipment. I was beside myself with agony for having missed the opportunity to attend. Soon my brother returned, wide-eyed and full of tales about everything he'd seen: real machine guns, real tracer bullets, real bazookas, plus parachutes with bright magnesium flares that lit up the target area. We lay awake that night plotting what we would do the next day. The demonstration had taken place about two miles south of town at a small community firing range next to the sawmill where my father and great-uncle worked. We had often tried to make parachutes, rather unsuccessfully, and were especially eager to get the parachutes before some other kids got them.

I was at that lucky age of thirteen and in the eighth grade, my last year of grammar school. Mike and I rode our bikes out as soon as possible the next morning. No one else had beaten us to the firing range. Our first find at the shooting area was some cardboard tubes with metal caps in which the bazooka shells had been transported. There were also heaps of brass shell casings from the machine guns. Out in the target area, a sawdust disposal heap from the nearby sawmill, we looked for but couldn't find any of the parachutes. But we eagerly scooped up 50-mm machine-gun bullet tips lying around on top of the sawdust, to be put together with their brass casings later. Then we found some fragments of exploded bazooka shells. Coming over a crest of sawdust, I saw lying before me a nearly perfect, olive drab, intact bazooka shell with only a bullet hole through its nose (Figure 1). I didn't hesitate to scoop it up and declare my ownership, while simultaneously peering through the hole. I was the luckiest boy alive! Immediately, Mike and I figured out what must have happened the night before: as the missile was winging its way through the air toward the target area, it had been hit by a stray round from a machine gun, and all its powder had drained out before it hit the soft sawdust. There was just one slight inexplicable problem: how did the bazooka shell get crossways to the machine-gun fire? (In fact, bazookas are designed as antitank weapons. In order to detonate, they must hit something very hard, such as a tank. The front half of the shell houses a vacuum chamber designed to implode and flatten out on the surface of the tank milliseconds before detonation. The firing pin is located in the central part of the front end of the shell, and the explosive charge is in the rear end of the head of the shell. My "dud" was completely live. When the naïve Guardsmen shot a bazooka that didn't explode on impact [because it hit soft sawdust!], they were concerned about leaving a live shell out there on a public shooting range, so they laid a belt of machine-gun fire back and forth in an effort to explode the bazooka shell from a safe distance. Evidently, they hit it once but that hit still failed to trip the firing pin [this is a cumulative device, with each impact moving it a little closer to detonation!]. None of the National Guardsmen was brave enough to go out to the target area in the dark looking for this dangerous bomb,

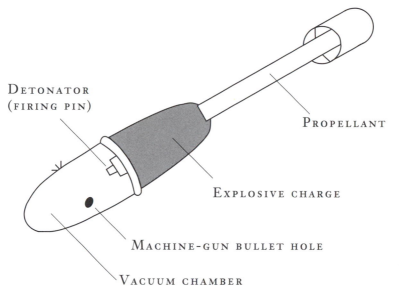

DETONATOR
(FIRING PIN)

PROPELLANT

EXPLOSIVE CHARGE

MACHINE-GUN BULLET HOLE

VACUUM CHAMBER

FIGURE 1
*Diagram of the
anatomy of a
Bazooka shell*

and they left it there for a lucky thirteen-year-old boy to find the next day.)

I planned to restore my trophy to its full original state by pounding back the metal flanges where the bullet had exited, soldering over the holes, and painting over the patches. We intended to hide in our foxholes in the field behind our house and fling the bazooka shell back and forth. Lovingly, I slid my bazooka shell into one of the cardboard tubes and screwed on the cap.

We had much too much loot to carry it all home on our bicycles, so we went up to the sawmill with it. We saw my great-uncle Emil and another mill worker piling lumber, and we showed them all our treasures. Then we found our father, foreman of the mill, too busy to examine our precious war toys just then. We asked him if we could put some stuff in the back seat of his car so that we wouldn't have to carry it all on our bikes. Preoccupied, he said something like, "Sure, go ahead." We piled it all into his car and rode home on our bikes. My scoutmaster, a local plumber, was doing some plumbing on an addition we were building on to our house. With great excitement, I told him about my find, and when my father came home for lunch, I retrieved my bazooka shell, pulled it out of its tube, and eagerly showed it to my scoutmaster. Proudly saying that he had shot bazookas during the war, my ex-veteran scoutmaster examined the shell, concurring that it had indeed been rendered harmless.

Soon thereafter, my brother called me to lunch. Mike was standing on the front porch, and I was about ten meters away in the front yard. I put my bazooka shell back into its tube again and gently let the long tube slide through my hand to the lawn below. When it hit the ground, it detonated. BOOM! I had been standing facing north at the time. The next thing I knew, I was lying on my back with my head pointing north. I sat up and looked in disbelief at my lower left leg, which was half gone and twisted at a nightmarish L-shaped angle, with my left foot off at a right angle from the leg to which it belonged. At first it was gray, but then it immediately exploded into vivid crimson, with blood gushing out in great spurts. My scoutmaster who was right there came to my rescue immediately, his military instincts functioning perfectly. He pushed my upper body down, whipped off his belt, and tightened it as a tourniquet around my left thigh (I was told later that if he hadn't done this so quickly I would have bled to death right there in our front yard). When my father came up, I said to him, "Why did you let me do it, Dad?" This thoughtless remark must have made him feel terrible, but it was really rather absurd since he hadn't given permission in any way—Mike and I had simply asserted our own freedom to do as we wished (to my parents' credit, we were given a lot of rope!). Blood was trickling down my face from cuts in my forehead. I noticed that the tip of my right middle finger had been hit, and about a third of the finger was flayed wide open to the bone. Within minutes the ambulance arrived, and I was loaded onto a stretcher and transported the two blocks to the Siskiyou County General Hospital.

I was in a state of shock. The first pain I felt was when the gurney was wheeled up a ramp headfirst, and the blood rushed to my decimated leg. All four of the town's doctors attended to me in surgery for nearly four hours that afternoon. One stitched up small head wounds and amputated the tip of my middle finger. The others tied off blood vessels and removed shrapnel; pieces of my jeans; and dead, powder-burned, damaged tissue. The front half of my lower left leg was gone, and there were gaping holes in the backside of the calf. A large chunk of flesh had been ripped out of my right thigh, but luckily the shrapnel missed the bone and did not sever any tendons on that leg. Ten centimeters of my left tibia (shinbone) had been blown away, and the smaller fibula was broken in two places. Most of the muscles and tendons were damaged. Three of the four local M.D.s were prepared to amputate my left leg then and there. But our family doctor, who had supervised the births of myself and all my siblings, felt that if he could just keep my leg on long enough to get me to a specialist he knew about in San Francisco, they might be able to save my leg. (Years later, after I broke my left leg the third time in an auto accident, another medical doctor said to me, "It isn't much, but it's the only left leg you're going to get. Take care of it!")

I awoke from my first surgery extremely sick to my stomach from the unfamiliar ether, in traction, with my left leg lying on a canvas cradle in a sort of sling, with a metal pin through my heel pulled by a window weight hanging on a pulley at the foot of the bed. Underneath the canvas sling was a pan. The front half of my leg was gone—it was like a piece of beefsteak with charred nubs of bone sticking out. They kept the raw muscles and nerves covered with gauze, squirting a saline solution on it with a big turkey baster every hour or so to keep it from drying out. The life-saving, but viscous and painful, penicillin shots began, every four hours, night and day, around the clock: 8:00 A.M., 12:00 noon, 4:00 P.M., 8:00 P.M., 12:00 midnight, 4:00 A.M., etc. "Time for your shot again, Ricky." I began to feel like a pincushion and got to where I wept and begged not to be poked again in my already painfully sore little buttocks and arms and legs. Gangrene quickly set in, and pieces of my beefsteak leg turned green. Daily, the doctors would come in, pull off the gauze (very painful!), and snip off little pieces of dead, gangrenous muscle (also painful). What was left of my leg began to stink—it was like being attached to a dead, rotting road-killed animal. In my shell-shocked state, I fantasized that I would somehow recover in time to go on the scout camping trip two months away (people humored me along in this fantasy). I have had more than a dozen close brushes with death during the last half century, but this was one of the closest (certainly by far the most painful!).

I was fascinated with my ruptured eardrum—I couldn't actually breathe through my ear, but by holding my nose I could blow air out of it! Later, I learned to make the most of my amputated middle finger—I can flick people the finger with a graded response, either the full finger by using my left hand or just a half finger by using my right hand. It's also fun to poke the stub into my nostril or ear, particularly in the presence of children. Kids are fascinated by my stub and want to know how I lost the tip of my finger. I have a whole line of stories about how I lost it, each one ending with "Would you like to know how I really lost it?" Once, I was a member of a

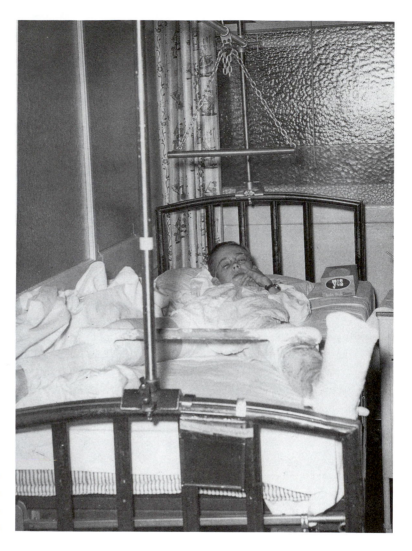

prestigious panel of herpetologists meeting to decide the future of herpetology. There were about eight of us sitting around a conference table. Glancing around, I noticed that about two-thirds of us had a missing digit. Herpetologists cannot resist picking up venomous snakes. Sooner or later, most manage to get bitten, and they often lose part of a digit in the process. I felt right at home in that group, even though I didn't lose mine to a snake (how were they to know?). Sometimes I wonder how much longer I will be able to avoid being bitten.

A full inquiry into the dreadful bazooka incident was made, of course. It turned out that the National Guardsmen concerned had illegally, and surreptitiously, taken the weapons away with them from their official training camp in order to recruit new members. Both Army and Marine officers visited me, marveling that I had survived a point blank bazooka blast, and they gave me a Purple Heart and a lieutenant colonel's silver oak-leaf badge. They concluded that I survived only because I was so close to the explosion that the shrapnel had not yet spread. These antitank weapons are designed to send shrapnel forward: 90 percent of the shrapnel blew down into the lawn, leaving a crater nearly a meter deep and a meter wide, and only about 10 percent blew back at me and everything else (the front side of our house had many broken windows and dozens of holes in it, my father's car looked like it had been strafed by machine-gun fire, and even a power line was cut). In the weeks following the blast, my dad picked up large pieces of my shinbone to keep the neighborhood dogs from eating them. Miraculously, no one else was injured. Pieces of shrapnel came quite close to hitting both my brother standing on the front porch and a visiting baby inside the house, but missed. To this day, I carry around several pieces that were not removed. Luckily, these are not big enough to set off the metal detectors at airports!

The nightmare continued for years. It was a long and arduous healing process, with bone grafts, skin grafts, tendon reconnections, Spica body casts, bedpans and bedsores, hospital beds, wheel chairs, leg braces, crutches, and so on. I must have been precariously close to becoming addicted to morphine at one point, for I remember lying there on a cloud in an exquisite euphoria begging for another pain shot (fortunately, the nurse would not give me one as enough time had not elapsed since the last one!).

Teenage boys are rambunctious: to lessen the boredom of being bedridden and isolated in cubicles in the pediatrics ward, another boy and I developed a harmless but entertaining game of "catch," throwing an empty small paper milk carton back and forth between our booths, over the cubicle wall. When we were discovered, a hard-nosed head nurse punished me by having me wheeled, bed and all, into solitary confinement for the remainder of the day (little did head nurse Lucille Ramsey know that she was contributing to the formation of a bona fide recluse and hermit!).

At some point, I lost my will to live. My appetite waned, and I wasted away, becoming extremely emaciated. The hospital's head dietician visited me and asked if there was anything I would eat. Other patients had to select their meals from a short menu, but I was encouraged to write in whatever I wished. I asked for pie, ice cream, strawberries, and watermelon out of season. But I did not gain weight, and I began to look like a victim of Auschwitz. Finally, the doctors decided to send me back home to my mother's cooking "to fatten me up" (we speculated that they wanted to get me stronger so that I could survive a leg amputation!). The long 350-mile trip by ambulance from San Francisco back to Yreka was a dream come true for me. Home again at last, my father weighed me in, cast and all, at only ninety pounds. We rented a hospital bed that could be cranked up and down with an overhead bar, and I took up residence in the front living room of our house, along with my urinal and bedpan. My mom's home cooking perked up my appetite; I devoured the familiar great food—rump roast, corn on the cob, mashed potatoes, and delicious noodles in rich beef gravy—and began to gain weight (in fact, I soon became overweight, bedridden as I was). My leg at this time was in a cast that was heavily discolored with blood and plasma, and for many months it still reeked rather like something dead. After six weeks, I returned to San Francisco to have the cast changed and the leg examined. Healing had been unexpectedly good.

A string of tiny pieces of periosteum deliberately left in place along the position of my former tibia eventually merged and began to rebuild a slightly shortened and crooked long bone. Unfortunately, I broke this fragile new piece of bone several years later and ended up in another body cast in high school. (My first year of high school was spent bedridden in a cast. A home teacher taught me English and typing.) This second break was a serious matter: eventually, it led to a pseudo-arthrosis (a "false joint") right in the middle of my tibia, which grew into a monstrous, painful knob before it finally managed to inhibit all movement enough for bone-to-bone connections to form once again. The knob has since receded and stopped being painful, but has left me with a crooked, partially paralyzed left leg about five centimeters shorter than my right leg. Legs of uneven length lead to spinal scoliosis (an S-shaped spine); this, coupled with bony vertebral spurs that develop naturally and inexorably with age (in response to "degenerative disk disease"), has left me in later life with a pinched nerve (in my neck) to my left arm. Because my left foot was kept tightly constrained in casts during critical years of growth, it remains about the size it was at age thirteen, a size 8 1/2, whereas my right foot grew to its full size, a size 11. Keeping myself in shoes and boots over the past four decades has been expensive (a wonderful agency, the National Odd Shoe Exchange, or N.O.S.E., pairs people up with their mis-mate, allowing shoe swaps).

Summers were usually devoted to reconstructive surgery, grafting skin and bone. At one point, to transfer a pellicle of flesh and skin from my right calf "donor area" to cover the extensive area of fragile thin scar tissue on my left leg, I actually had my legs sewn together for nearly two months. Sometime during this period, a medical doctor had to remove stitches from an inflamed area on my right leg near the bone. When he tugged on a stitch to pull it up so that he could snip it, a sharp pain shot up deep inside my leg, like a red-hot ramrod had been jabbed up the center of my leg. I yelled and told him that he couldn't do that, that it was incredibly painful, but he persisted and said just one more try. It took many more tries, each one unendurable, before the insensitive brute finally managed to cut and remove that unfortunate stitch, which must have been looped right around one of the branches of my sciatic nerve itself.

I will never forget the first time I was ordered to try to stand up (on crutches, of course), after being bed- and wheel-chair-ridden for over a year: the blood rushed to both legs, and they stung and swelled (to combat this, I wrapped them in Ace bandages, gradually loosening the wrap as I reacquired muscle tone). But what I remember most is feeling as if I was teetering on top of great stilts, so high, and so precariously perched. I had almost completely lost my sense of balance. My left knee wouldn't lock and just kept going backward on me, so they installed a knee latch lock on my leg brace (eventually, knee surgery restored my knee function to normal). They relocated the tendon that one uses to move the ankle side to side so that I could use it to achieve a tiny bit of lift (having lost all the muscles and tendons in the front side of my left leg, I have a permanently paralyzed "drop foot"). When the bone doctors proposed chopping out a 5-cm section of the femur of my right leg to equalize leg lengths, I vetoed the plan, declaring that I had already had enough surgery to last me for the rest of my life (also, I am long-torsoed and short-legged anyway, and I did not want to take any chances with my "good" right leg!).

I actually developed a sort of love-hate relationship with my own leg! More than once I would have willingly chosen death over the pain I had to suffer. But liabilities can be transformed into assets—from all that hardship and suffering emerged no small measure of endurance and strength: I learned to tolerate physical discomfort, became self-reliant, developed fortitude and independence, as well as an astonishingly strong will, all of which helped me to become a successful field biologist. Even before the bazooka-shell experience, I was a shy and introverted kid. Being crippled during my entire adolescence really prevented me from ever becoming "properly" socialized. Perhaps this, coupled with the long and lonely stints in the hospitals far away from home, contributed to my becoming inward oriented, somewhat of a recluse and a hermit. To this day I can be comfortable without company for extended periods of time, something that most of my friends cannot fathom (indeed, most of them say it would drive them crazy!). Certainly the unpleasant events in my childhood predisposed me to become a desert rat.

My injury actually had other advantages as well. When I turned eighteen, the draft board issued me medically disabled 4F status, which kept me from mandatory military service (I already had my war injuries and a Purple Heart!). My disabilities did not prevent me from putting many, many kilometers on that game leg, and I have led a very rewarding life in spite of it. Our lawsuit was eventually settled—Crippled Children's hospital, doctors' debts, and attorneys' fees paid off—and when I turned twenty-one, I came into enough money to buy a car and to pay for my graduate education.

As a sophomore in high school, a plump gimp on crutches, I joined the American Society of Ichthyologists and Herpetologists as a life member. All through this trying period, I had nurtured a dream, a plan for the future. When I graduated from high school, I was going to take my brother (he was my "legs") and go to Mexico to catch snakes and lizards. My parents humored me in this fantasy, probably thinking that it would never come to be. But I persisted, and planned it all out. Besides typing, Spanish, and English, the most important class I took in high school was auto shop: my class project involved overhauling the engine in my old brown 1948 DeSoto (auto mechanical skills should be a prerequisite for anyone who intends to survive fieldwork in remote areas). I worked and saved every cent I could for the trip.

My mother, Gini, was truly remarkable and exceedingly supportive. She didn't particularly like snakes, let alone venomous ones, yet she always encouraged me to follow my interests wherever they took me. I was allowed to keep Esmeralda, a five-foot boa constrictor, in

Rick on crutches in back yard (Yreka, about 1953)

the house. How many mothers would allow their teenage son to chill a live rattlesnake in the family refrigerator to cool it down for photography? Her only condition was that she wasn't going to enter the kitchen, let alone open the fridge, until I declared it "all clear."

Gini worked as a county librarian and saved enough on her meager salary to buy a set of four new tires for our journey. Right after high school graduation in early June of 1956, armed with our father's

FIGURE 2
U. S. and Mexican
travel routes

Standard Oil credit card—gasoline was 25 to 30 cents a gallon then—and about $200 in cash plus a letter of consent from our parents, Mike and I did indeed set out for Mexico. I wanted to catch a wild boa constrictor and an iridescent blue *Morpho* butterfly. My brother Mike wanted to buy, and explode, fireworks. He was fifteen, and I was seventeen, on crutches, and in a leg brace. We were both exceedingly naïve. This was when I discovered deserts—vast, magnificent, uninhabited, and unfenced stretches in Nevada, Arizona, and northern Mexico. Galloping along over the sagebrush to get a lizard jar from the car, I put a crutch down on a prairie rattlesnake. When it buzzed, even on crutches, I jumped sky high! Over a two-month period, we traveled some 9,200 miles through ten states in the U.S. plus another ten states in Mexico (Figure 2). We drove to Mexico City, where we caught turista and witnessed a genuine bullfight, then went south another 200 miles, on to Veracruz, never finding a boa constrictor (though Mike did manage to capture one of those strong, fast-flying morpho butterflies).

Late one evening, at the farthest point south of Mexico City that we reached on that expedition, the DeSoto suddenly began running very rough. We pulled into a gasoline station, I opened the hood and was dismayed to find water pouring out of the carburetor! The car soon died and obviously would not start, so we pushed it away from the pumps and rolled it down a little hill where we slept that night inside the locked car. From the symptoms, I knew it must be either a cracked head, a cracked block, or a blown head gasket. Early the next day, I pulled off the head. It was an enormous relief to discover that it was only a blown gasket, for I could not have repaired a cracked head or block and would have had to abandon my car in Mexico. I removed the blown gasket, left Mike to guard the car, and crutched my way a kilometer or so to the tiny Mexican village of Tehuacan (see Figure 2 inset). There was no auto parts store and only one small general store. Walking in on my crutches, I felt certain that they wouldn't have any auto parts, let alone the head gasket I needed. As luck would have it, my old car was just the vintage of most of the cars that Mexican nationals drove then. Also, luckily for me, almost all Chrysler products in those days used the same engine. I handed the clerk my blown gasket, and in my best high school Spanish said something like "¿Tiene ustay este?" (Do you have this?). He looked up high on the far wall at a selection of half a dozen copper head gaskets hanging from nails and walked over to a ladder. My gasket matched perfectly with the second one he tried! It cost only 31 pesos (U.S. $2.50). Needless to say, I was exceedingly fortunate to be able to buy that gasket—we were on the road again within a few hours, heading northward back to the good old United States of America. We ran off the road on the way and had to hire a tow truck. We had barely enough money to make it back to the border: I'll never forget arriving at a toll bridge to the United States that asked for "50¢"; if it was centavos we had it, but if it was U.S. cents we didn't!

On our return trip to Yreka, we drove through Texas, where one night as I crawled inside my sleeping bag I felt something fuzzy against my leg which turned out to be a tarantula (next to my face by flashlight, this spider looked immense!). We spent the remainder of that night sleeping on top of roadside picnic tables. In Louisiana, we rented a small rowboat and looked for, but could not find, a wild alligator, although we did catch some *Anolis*. Two policemen stopped us, wondering what two kids were doing driving a car with California plates over a thousand miles away from home—I think they would have taken us in if I hadn't been able to produce that letter giving us parental permission! When I told them I was looking for water moccasins, they looked at one another and then at me like I must be crazy. We drove through Missouri, Kansas, Nebraska, Wyoming, Utah, and Nevada and saw Yellowstone National Park and the Great Salt Lake on the way. By now, I could hobble short distances without my crutches using a cane. We stopped at every roadside snake pit and snake farm, and at one in Texas, I bought several small diamondback rattlesnakes and an indigo snake, alive but emaciated, which soon died and were pickled. At one such place, there was a pair of cobras in an unattended and unlocked cage—I opened the cage and prodded them with my cane to get the snakes to hood. It frightened my brother, but I found it thrilling! At long last, we returned to Yreka, more mature, well-traveled, and wiser, but flat broke. I had to sell the trustworthy old DeSoto for a mere $100.

From there I went off by bus on a long journey to Carleton College, a small liberal arts school about forty miles south of Minneapolis, Minnesota, where I spent the four coldest winters of my life, and began my education. During the summer between my sophomore and junior years, I made a second trip through Mexico all the way into Guatemala with my best college buddy and his friend. On that six-week journey, I managed to make a small collection of snakes and lizards, most of them road-killed animals (D.O.R.'s: dead on road). During my junior year, I published my first scientific paper, a brief note describing that Mexican collection. At that time, my life's goal was to write a definitive book on the reptiles of Mexico (such a book is much needed but still has not been done by anyone!). Although I did finally get rid of the leg brace, I stayed on crutches the whole time I was at Carleton, majoring in biology without discovering my specialty. I was just a C student as a freshman, but by my senior year I had almost straight A's. However, my record wasn't good enough to gain admission to the really first-rate graduate schools such as Berkeley, Stanford, and Harvard.

In the summer following my graduation from Carleton, I was stunned to find myself denied admission to all the graduate schools to which I had aspired. So I hastily applied to three lesser institutions, all in the Pacific Northwest. That summer, while I awaited acceptances or rejections, my other brother Nick and I packed in and camped out for three weeks at a high mountain lake in the Marble Mountains (later designated an official Wilderness Area). One night we heard a cougar's shrill cry. This was when I first allowed my beard to grow out—I have now worn it steadily for over thirty years. I still remember the return to civilization as a jarring experience, hearing cars and other unpleasant noises of human origin for the first time in weeks. Being in the wilderness spoils you so that cities actually become distasteful.

The good news was that I had been admitted (although it was too late for any financial aid) to all three of the northwestern graduate schools. I chose to attend the one that was farthest from home, the University of Washington at Seattle (which at that time did not enjoy nearly as prestigious an academic reputation as it now does). The transition to graduate school was when I metamorphosed from "Rick" to "Eric"; I finally discarded my crutches, which had become a part of me, a sort of security blanket; and I also began wearing contact lenses. My limp gave me character that set me apart from my fellow graduate students! To set up my own household in graduate school, I inherited an old gray wool blanket that my uncle had brought back from the Second World War—it had a small white tag that said Made in Australia. Over the next several years, this blanket came to symbolize a dream, another dream that I eventually managed to make come true.

In graduate school, I became interested in the problem of species diversity: why are there more species in some places than in others?

A prominent geographical pattern, repeated in many different groups of plants and animals, became the focus of my research: latitudinal gradients in species diversity. I chose to study the ecology and diversity of flatland desert lizards in western North America, along a 1,000-km latitudinal transect from southern Idaho through southern Arizona (Figure 3). For three field seasons, I was a desert rat, living out of a blue Volkswagen van fondly called Elizabeth (Betsy, for short), driving up and down this transect collecting data. Five years later I finished my Ph.D. I found that the number of species of lizards living together in flatland desert habitats varied from four species in the cold shrubby deserts in the north to as many as ten species in the warm Sonoran desert in southern Arizona. The number of species of lizards occurring together was correlated with the structural complexity and spatial heterogeneity of the vegetation in desert habitats. Northern deserts support a homogeneous vegetation consisting of small chenopodiaceous shrubs, such as sagebrush and saltbush (*Atriplex*). Southern deserts, in contrast, support a much more complex vegetation which includes a variety of small semi-shrubs, larger woody shrubs including creosote bush (*Larrea*), scattered trees such as Joshua "trees," palo verde, and ironwood, plus various sorts of cactus. Several species of climbing lizards require large shrubs and trees.

When I began my fieldwork in the early 1960s, the U.S. desert southwest was still pretty much wide open and unfenced. One could pull off the road virtually anywhere and find relatively pristine desert. This gradually changed with the encroachment of urbanization, grazing, agriculture, and land speculation. By the next decade, unfenced desert had become very hard to find.

While working on my Ph.D. dissertation, I conceived of an ideal follow-up research project: namely, to compare an independently evolved desert-lizard system with the one I had just studied. I had already begun to dream about the possibility of one day emigrating to Australia, and so it was natural to propose as a postdoctoral project the comparison of Australian desert lizards with those in North America. I applied for, and was awarded, a three-year stipend as a National Institutes of Health postdoctoral fellow to work with the world's leading ecologist, the late Professor Robert H. MacArthur, at Princeton University. In November of 1965, I went to Princeton and wrote a companion proposal to the National Science Foundation to support the proposed fieldwork in Australia (this was also funded, for

Great Basin

L
•
G
•

I
•

V
•

P
•

Mojave

M
•

S
•

T
•

W
•

C
•

Sonoran

A
•

B
•

0   200   500
KILOMETERS

FIGURE 3
U. S. study sites
(plus two in Mexico).
Approximate
boundaries of various
deserts in western
North America are
also shown.

Newlyweds Helen and Eric (Yreka, Christmas 1965)

MacArthur agreed to be a co-principal investigator). In December, I flew out to the West Coast, married Helen, a graduate school colleague—now my ex-wife—and we attended the American Association for the Advancement of Science (AAAS) meetings at the University of California at Berkeley, where I presented a paper in a session on diversity, along with MacArthur and others.

Springtime found me back in Seattle, typing up Helen's Ph.D. thesis. We spent part of May and June 1966 driving brutal dirt roads half the length of Baja California, then a real wilderness area (before the paved highway was constructed). We undertook to census lizards on low shrubby flat desert areas, comparable to other sites I had studied earlier farther north. We found a flatland desert site in Baja that was structurally comparable to my study sites in the Great Basin, with five different species of lizards coexisting together. At any given site in the flatland deserts of western North America, the exact number of lizard species present depends primarily on the structural complexity and spatial heterogeneity of the vegetation. I expected to find similar patterns in Australian deserts. I was especially interested in making detailed comparisons of so-called ecological equivalents, independently evolved lineages that occupy roughly the same ecological roles on different continents. A prime example would be North American horned lizards, which are in a different family than their Australian counterpart the thorny devil. Such products of convergent evolution are of special interest to biologists because they suggest that natural selection favors predictable responses to particular environmental exigencies. Moreover, the existence of such convergent species pairs indicates that evolutionary pathways can be predictable and repeatable. I had hopes not only of documenting such evolutionary convergence in detail but also perhaps of contributing new ideas about the vital process of natural selection itself.

In July of 1966, Helen and I boarded a German freighter, aptly named the *Cap Finisterre* ("end of the earth!"), and sailed under the Golden Gate and out across the Pacific on our great adventure down under. Having read some of Somerset Maugham's stories that took place while traveling on freighters, we expected to have very interesting shipmates. Also, going by ship enabled us to take much more luggage than we would have been allowed if we had flown. Everyone should undertake such an ocean trip, if for no other reason than to gain a real appreciation for the vastness of planet Earth. Flying fish sail through the air between waves, occasionally landing on the pitching deck. The huge ship dips, and climbs waves the size of small hills. Water crashes over the bow. At twelve o'clock sharp each noon, the ship's navigator shot the sun's azimuth with his sextant and plotted with a colored pin his estimate of our exact position on a huge map of the Pacific Ocean posted on the wall in a central social area outside the dining room. Powered by giant cylinders the size of fifty-gallon drums, the great ship crashed along at fifteen knots or so night and day, but we crept across the Pacific at an agonizingly slow pace

(I not only was anxious to get to Australia but also found that I get seasick—I am a landlubber!). It's hard to sleep with the boat pitching and yawing, threatening to throw you right out of your bunk!

Crossing the equator and entering the Southern Hemisphere for the first time was properly celebrated with the time-honored, famous ceremony of Neptune's (we also crossed the international date line and lost a full day!). To help pass time aboard ship, we read many Australian novels, such as Neville Shute's *A Town Like Alice* and *In the Wet*, and Arthur Upfield's *Death of a Lake*, *The Will of the Tribe*, and *Bony and the Black Virgin*. After a brief stopover in Tahiti to unload lumber from the Pacific Northwest, we finally made port in Sydney, a full three and a half weeks after departing from San Francisco. It was awfully good to reach land again. I guess I must have finally gotten my "sea legs," but I was hardly prepared for the inverse side of sea sickness: for a little while right after you get off a long stint on a ship at open sea, it actually feels as if the solid ground on which you stand is pitching to and fro like the ship's deck to which you have become so accustomed!

Upon arrival in Australia, the entire ship was placed under quarantine until a medical doctor came on board and everyone aboard passed health inspection. They looked especially for an outbreak of smallpox at sea. Australia still has no rabies or hoof-and-mouth disease, and authorities are doing their best to keep such fatal diseases off the island continent. It used to be the case that when you arrived down under by jet at the Sydney airport, no one was allowed to get up until authorities had walked up and down the aisles, both hands spraying aerosol canisters of insecticide above the heads of all passengers (I'm glad they have now discontinued this rather noxious procedure).

Disembarking in Sydney, I injured my lower back loading a large and very heavy trunk filled with most of our worldly possessions, including books and tools, into a taxicab (the driver wisely refused to assist me). The mild Australian climate allows all sorts of improbable plants to be grown outside, things such as poinsettias and hibiscus, which one normally thinks of as potted plants that must be kept inside (Australian gardens are somewhat akin to a florist's shop).

A year and a half later, we returned stateside on an American freighter, the SS *Sonoma* of the Matson Lines, stopping in Samoa and Hawaii. Since then, I have flown across the Pacific several times (and have learned that QANTAS stands for Queensland and Northern

Territory Aerial Services!). The long and grueling twenty-plus-hour flight has always seemed quite trivial by comparison with the journey on the surface! At least when you go by ship, you don't suffer from jet lag!

Getting accustomed to the strong Australian accent and learning a new vocabulary are two of the problems one first encounters down under. A book called *Les Stalk Strine* (Let's talk Australian) translated air conditioner as "egg nitioner." For northeast, they say "noreast." "Bali" becomes "barley." Thirteen is "thirdeen," eighteen is "aighteen," etc. Like the English, Aussies have different words for many things: sick or ill is "crook," expensive is "dear," stolen is "pinched," a chicken is a "chook," supper is "tea," gasoline is "petrol" ("gas" refers to propane), kerosene is "paraffin," a car's hood is its "bonnet," the windshield is the "windscreen," good day is "g'die," anyone of the opposite sex is "love," and so on.

Another nontrivial problem is learning to look to the right, rather than to the left, before crossing a street (like the British from whom they descended, Aussies still drive on the left-hand side of the road). Every time I change continents, I nearly kill myself because my reflexes have become trained to look the other way! (I also tend to want to drive on the "wrong" side of the road! People give you some really strange looks when they see you chugging merrily along on the wrong side.) Laws and attitudes toward pedestrians and jaywalking differ markedly from those in the States. In Australia, pedestrians have absolute autonomy in marked crosswalks—people scurry to rush out in front of oncoming traffic, which must screech to a halt, and stay stopped, until everyone is out of the crosswalk. On the other hand, in Australia, away from marked crosswalks, vehicles always have the right-of-way. Once, I raced across the main street of Kalgoorlie, inadvertently forcing an accelerating car to reduce speed a little—a big, burly Aussie shook his fist at me, yelling "Damned Yanks!" Law-abiding Aussies would never jaywalk if it might cause traffic to slow. And most vehicle drivers drive without courtesy to pedestrians, as if they damn well know that they have the right-of-way.

It takes a while to assimilate the concept that the sun is in the north at midday (at first, it seems as if east and west somehow got reversed). I encountered an astronomical mystery down under, too. It's a foreground-background problem. The same old familiar moon rises in the east, floats high in the sky, and sets in the west, going through its lunar cycle from new moon to full moon more or less as it does in the Northern Hemisphere. But both the moon and the starry background behind it are actually upside down—people in the two hemispheres are, quite literally, feet to feet! Much of the celestial background is totally different. Instead of the Big Dipper, one sees the emblem of Australia, the Southern Cross. How can the same moon be in the foreground against such different backgrounds? I have a pretty good three-dimensional perspective, but I just can't seem to manage to visualize or get comfortable with the geometry of this paradoxical situation—perhaps I need to see a good model!

Australians have gone hog-wild for bureaucracy: one must obtain a permit to do just about anything. As in Great Britain, there are very strong gun-control laws, and ordinary individuals are not allowed to possess handguns (criminals have them, of course). Pistols are not imported into Australia and cannot be purchased there. As .22-caliber revolvers were essential tools for my research, I had made inquiries about what to do and had been advised to bring them over with me, and to make application for special dispensation upon arrival. The weapons were seized by customs upon arrival, pending firing tests and police permission. It took some doing, but eventually the authorities allowed me to license two revolvers to be used only for collecting lizards with dust shot, and only in the outback. I was surprised to find that I also had to register spring-loaded BB guns, which I had always considered "toys" but which the Aussie police classified as "air rifles." Permits are also necessary to collect lizards, and nowadays one must have a "vivisectionist's license" as well. Just to be on certain tracks requires several special permits from various authorities. You are supposed to have a license to look for gold or minerals (which belong to the Crown), as well as to have a dog or a bicycle. Australians seem to have a penchant for red tape. For a nation descended from a bunch of transported convicts, Aussies have become a pretty law-abiding lot! In reality, however, there is next to no enforcement of Australia's multitudinous laws in the outback. The single game warden ("Wildlife Officer") charged with enforcing laws protecting the fauna of the largest district in Western Australia (about half a million square kilometers) is allocated a mere 1,000 kilometers per week for travel.

A few months before departing from the U.S., we had sold both our cars and sunk literally every cent we had (and then some, borrowing from the savings of trusting loyal friends) into the purchase of a four-wheel-drive Land Rover station wagon—complete with an extra fuel tank, a tropical roof, winch, and British license plates—directly from the factory in Great Britain on an overseas delivery plan, scheduled to be delivered to the docks at Sydney shortly before we were to arrive.[2] The ship carrying the vehicle from England was delayed several weeks, giving us ample time to locate camping equipment, a used Royal Flying Doctor Service (RFDS) transceiver, etc. An exceedingly hospitable Australian couple we had met on the freighter graciously invited us to stay with them during this waiting period. Our fine new field vehicle, soon christened "Matilda,"[3] finally arrived, and one fine day in the early Austral spring (August), we took possession of our blue Land Rover. I had a near miss at the docks, almost crushing my skull when I allowed the hood, weighted down by a heavy spare tire, to fall on my head (I was used to the American spring-loaded and cantilevered hoods and didn't expect it to drop like a lead weight!). Packing everything up and saying good-bye to our generous Australian friends, we headed westward for the great Australian deserts.

NOTES TO CHAPTER 1

1. Many of the species mentioned in this book have no common names and will thus be referred to by their scientific name, a Latin binomial.

2. Because Australia has stiff import duties, we ordered an American style car with the steering wheel on the left side, with the intent of getting the vehicle into the country on a temporary basis by guaranteeing that we would export it at the end of our stay. This way we could have the car back in the United States for as long as we wanted. To import it into Australia required posting a bond to guarantee the duty. We also had to sport a large sign on the rear of the vehicle that said CAUTION: LEFT-HAND DRIVE. Australia has now outlawed such vehicles precisely because they constitute a road hazard.

3. "Matilda" was an apt name because it refers to a person's "swag," which is a bundle containing all one's belongings. The swagman in "Waltzing Matilda" is carrying his bundle of possessions on his back. Our Matilda carried everything we had and was our life-support system!

TRAVELING

Two

IT WAS A GOOD THING THAT NEITHER OF US HAD DRIVEN for months. It took some doing to get used to driving on the other side of the road. Driving was especially difficult with the driver sitting in the gutter on the outside edge of the road. Luckily there were two of us, for it would have been next to impossible to pass ("overtake" down under) without the help of a passenger sitting in the "driver's" seat! There wasn't much traffic. Main roads were paved for the first half of the trip, but the pavement ended somewhere in South Australia. The Eyre Highway across the Nullarbor Plain was then only a dirt road stretching for many hundred kilometers, full of mudholes and deep ruts (Figure 4). Virtually every time we pulled off the road for lunch or to camp or whatever, almost every passing vehicle would slow down, stop, and someone would shout out, "You right, mite?" (translation: "Are you all right, mate?"—a common modern saying is "She'll be right" meaning something like "Everything will be O.K."). This extreme hospitality was surprising but a bit of a nuisance at times. Eventually, we learned to pull far away from the road whenever we stopped so as not to attract attention.

We did not see very many lizards on that first trip across the continent, but we did see many kangaroos and a few wombats, plus lots of exotic and beautiful birds. In the center of the Eyre "highway," I was pleased to find a live death adder, an elapid snake ecologically equivalent to vipers and pit vipers, but a fixed-fang snake related to cobras (this proved to be the only death adder I would see in four years in the outback).

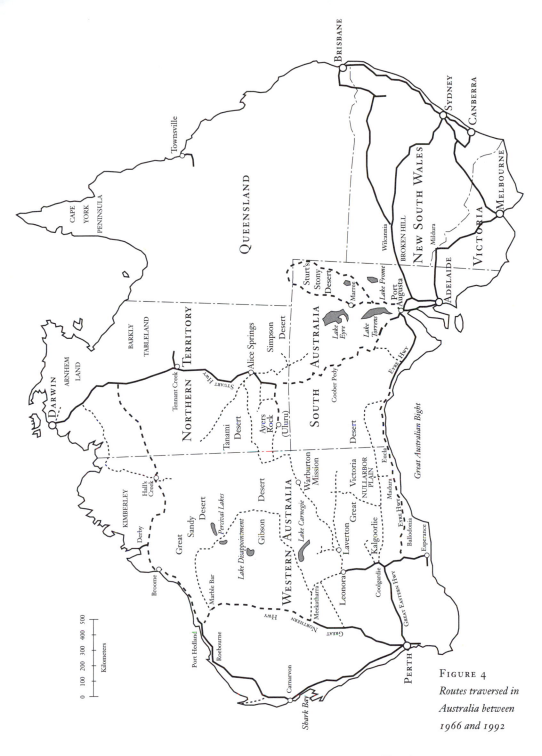

CAPE
YORK
PENINSULA

Townsville

QUEENSLAND

DARWIN

ARNHEM
LAND

KIMBERLEY

BARKLY
TABLELAND

NORTHERN TERRITORY

Tennant Creek

STUART HWY

Alice Springs

Tanami
Desert

Ayers
Rock
(Uluru)

Simpson
Desert

SOUTH AUSTRALIA

Sturt's
Stony
Desert

Marree

Lake
Eyre

Lake
Torrens

Lake Frome

Port
Augusta

Wilcannia

BROKEN HILL

NEW SOUTH WALES

Mildura

BRISBANE

SYDNEY

CANBERRA

MELBOURNE

VICTORIA

ADELAIDE

Coober Pedy

Eyre Hwy

Great Australian Bight

Hall's
Creek

Derby

Great
Sandy
Desert

Percival Lakes

Lake Disappointment

Gibson
Desert

WESTERN AUSTRALIA

Warburton
Mission

Lake Carnegie

Victoria
Desert

Great
NULLARBOR
PLAIN

Eucla

Madura

Eyre Hwy

Ballodonia

Esperance

Broome

Marble Bar

Meekatharra

Laverton

Leonora

Kalgoorlie

Coolgardie

NORTHERN HWY

GREAT EASTERN HWY

Port Hedland

Roebourne

Carnarvon

Shark Bay

PERTH

0 100 200 300 400 500

Kilometers

FIGURE 4
Routes traversed in
Australia between
1966 and 1992

Traveling

When, a couple of weeks later, we arrived, tired and dusty, in Perth, one of the most isolated and delightful cities in the world, we were already beginning to become relatively seasoned bush travelers (but, as you will see, I continued to make many more mistakes!). I soon found my Australian sponsor, Professor A. R. Main, in the library at the Department of Zoology at the University of Western Australia. He cautioned me that what I wanted to do would be extremely difficult, if not impossible, and gave me some good advice about traveling in the outback, such as to carry lots of spare parts, an air compressor, and a high-lift, long-handled "wallaby" jack. Next I visited the curator of herpetology at the Western Australian Museum, the late Dr. Glen Storr, who suggested taking shovels and a rake. Storr explained to us the art of finding nocturnal geckos by using headlights to detect the faint glow of their eyeshine. He also described many other techniques for collecting lizards, including burning spinifex grass tussocks as a way to obtain some species that are difficult or impossible to get in any other way.

Australia is approximately the size of the continental United States. It is rough, wild country, and it's difficult to get from here to there. Aussies have a saying, "the tyranny of distance," which refers to the fact that it takes a long while for anything to get anywhere within, into, or out of Australia. We had little or no idea of where to go, and neither did anyone else. So we had to undertake some serious exploration at the outset. Virtually no ecological work had ever been undertaken in the vast central deserts. The first thing to do was to drive all the major "highways" (in 1966, most of these were still unpaved dirt roads). Many thousands of kilometers and months later, I came to realize that all these major roads skirted the real sandy deserts, which occupy roughly half the continent's surface area, and which turned out to be far and away the most interesting habitats for studies of lizard ecology. However, to reach the sandy deserts, one has to take unmaintained, little-used, or abandoned side "tracks" and put oneself at risk due to extreme isolation. (A colleague of mine traveled 50,000 km throughout Australia and never even saw the red sand desert country!)

I constructed a spacious top carrier to allow us to carry extra gear. We stocked up on supplies in Perth and followed the Great Northern Highway a thousand kilometers north to the Indian Ocean, crossing the Tropic of Capricorn, then across the top end of Western Australia through the southern part of the Kimberley. Along the way

we found an echidna (a primitive egg-laying mammal related to the duck-billed platypus and known as a monotreme) as well as our first *Varanus gouldi* (a monitor lizard), the latter over a meter in length. After capturing and marveling at the beast, we took pictures before releasing it. The washboards, or "corrugations," in the "highway" loosened nuts and bolts and nearly tore the Land Rover apart. Our route took us through Meekatharra, Marble Bar, Port Hedland, Broome, Derby, and Hall's Creek (see Figure 4).

Another close brush with death came unexpectedly one hot day. We stopped at a roadside fuel station, and while Helen went off to the toilet, I began refilling about half a dozen five-gallon jerricans with gasoline. Stupidly, I had completely forgotten about the little gas flame in our small propane refrigerator that was cooling drinks up front in Matilda. Suddenly, there was a *ka whomp!* of blue flame, and I looked down to see a full open jerrican of petrol merrily burning away. Quickly, I clamped down the lid, depriving the fire of air. Then two blokes came running up, one released the emergency brake, and we pushed Matilda, rolling her away from the pumps into a ditch

Crossing the tropic heading north

Helen with a spiny anteater, or echidna

some distance away. Luckily, there were no more explosions. When Helen emerged from the ladies room and found out what an idiot I had been, she was furious—she had nearly come out to no husband, no possessions, and sheer and utter desolation in a foreign country! Every time I see some jerk mindlessly puffing away on a cigarette right next to gasoline pumps sporting bright red No Smoking signs, I shudder as I remember my own folly.

Lialis burtonis,
a crepuscular
snakelike flap-
footed lizard that
feeds on skinks

Fascinating baobab "bottle" trees, reminiscent of those in Africa, greeted us in the southern Kimberley. These drought-resistant hollow trees store water. One fine warm night, we camped looking out over the Indian Ocean on the Eighty Mile Beach, which at that time was not only pristine but completely devoid of any other people. Nowadays one could never enjoy that experience, as the beach is cluttered with people and debris. As an added bonanza, I caught my first pygopodid lizard, a legless flap-footed *Lialis burtonis*. This interesting lizard is a predator of skinks (lizards that protect themselves with bony plates called osteoderms embedded in each scale). Like skink-eating snakes, *Lialis* has evolved hinged teeth that fold back, enabling them to get a better purchase on skinks (an excellent example of convergent evolution and ecological equivalence).

One of the novels we had read on the ship centered around an interesting place called Wolf Creek Meteorite Crater on the northern edge of the Great Sandy Desert. Since this crater was marked on the map only about 50–100 km south of the main road, we decided to go see it (I also wanted to see the Great Sandy Desert). The track quickly deteriorated to nothing, but I bravely decided to continue cross-country. (Matilda was the first four-wheel-drive vehicle I had ever owned, and I naïvely thought she could go anywhere—I have since learned the hard way that high technology only gets you stuck worse.) We had two spare tires, one mounted on the bonnet, and the other low on the outside of the rear door. Trying to cross over a dippy

little wash, the rear spare tire hung up when the rear wheels dropped down into the ditch. The door was sprung and rather badly bent by this, the first serious damage to our now-not-so-brand-new Land Rover. (It was a design flaw to mount the tire so low!) The gaping hole at the bottom of the back door sucked in dust churned up from underneath the car. Thoroughly disgusted, we turned back, never finding that meteorite crater, the second largest in the world. At camp that evening, I took the tire off the bent door, removed the door from Mat, and used the tire jack to try to bend it back to some semblance of its original normal shape, then reassembled everything. However, much to our chagrin, the fit remained too loose and continued to suck in dust.

As luck would have it, over the next few days we encountered vast stretches of what Aussies call "bull dust," extremely fine, talcum-powder-like dust churned up by passing vehicles. In some stretches, the stuff was literally centimeters deep! When it rains, this powdery dust turns to instant slimy, slippery mud. Bull dust got sucked up around the loosely-fitted bent rear door and filled the inside of the vehicle until we had to gasp for breath. We had grit in our hair, our skin pores, our bed, our clothes, and our food. "Road trains," huge

trucks pulling several trailers in tandem, left behind them a dense cloud of bull dust hanging in the air for what seemed to be kilometers! It got so bad that when I saw one of these trucks coming the other way, I pulled off the track several hundred meters on the upwind side and waited for the dust to settle before proceeding.

Matilda plows through the bull dust.

Northern Australia can be a stark, eerie, dead place in the "dry" (an Aussie term for the dry season). Forests of standing skeletons of long-dead mulga trees, bleached as white as bones by the intense sunlight, extended for many kilometers, interspersed with graveyards of thousands of tombstone-like termitaria jutting up to a meter above ground. There are stories of termites destroying entire buildings in northern Australia. At dusk, camped alongside a windmill and at a cattle water tank, dozens of flying foxes, enormous megachiropteran bats, descended, flying in great circles, periodically dropping one at a time to the surface of the tank to fetch a drink on the wing. With a wingspread of a half meter, these are far and away the biggest bats in the world. Some biologists once thought that the megachiropterans might actually be closer to primates than to the other small bats, the microchiropterans! If so, flight would have evolved twice among mammals, and these two groups would be highly convergent.

Stark, eerie forests of long dead trees in the Kimberley

At Hall's Creek, I pulled up alongside the petrol pumps, horrified at the outrageously high price but resolved to pay it, got out, and waited for an attendant. Many minutes passed but no one came, so I finally went inside and asked for help. A bloke may have nodded, but otherwise ignored me. After standing around for another fifteen minutes, I had had enough and departed angrily, stopping down the road a bit to refill from my own jerrican reserve. (Later I learned that in such remote places one is expected to sit down, have a few beers, and shoot the breeze for an hour or so, and then they finally get around to asking about refilling petrol tanks. My American impatience never did mesh well with rural Australia.)

A few days later, we were relieved to reach the Stuart Highway, at that time the only sealed road in the entire Northern Territory. Paved by the Americans during the Second World War as a response to the threat of a Japanese invasion, this road links Alice Springs with Darwin. We went south to Alice and the "red center" (the interior two-thirds of Australia), made quick trips into the Tanami and Simpson deserts, plus a visit to Ayers Rock and The Olgas. We found some nice lizards, but no place quite good enough to designate a study area. To return west, I tried to cross the continent via a little-used track from South Australia through the Great Victoria Desert directly to Western Australia, but when an Emu Downs station person told me that no one was allowed to use this "restricted" track, we returned to Perth along the Eyre Highway knowing full well what to expect the second time.

Large flocks of pink-and-gray Galah Cockatoos were often feeding on the verge along the edge of the highway. We needed a mascot. Cockatoos are supposed to make excellent pets, so we felt that this would be an ideal opportunity to find out. I climbed up to a Galah nest and took a tiny little chick not much bigger than a newly hatched chicken. His eyes were open but he was a funny-looking little bird. As patriotic Americans (by this time we were getting a little homesick), we christened him Benjamin Franklin. Helen mixed up a concoction of sunflower seeds, oatmeal, nuts, and flour, which we forced down him. But only for a little while, because Ben grew fast, and he quickly learned to eat. He imprinted on us and thought he was a human, I think.

Ben would sit on one of our shoulders, rubbing his head against our cheek, squawking and cackling, whistling and preening. He got very excited when one of us whistled back at him! When Ben's flight feathers grew in, we trimmed the tip of one wing a little so that he wouldn't be able to fly away too easily, but left enough so that he could still fly. He had his perch, and he loved to sit on one of our shoulders and nibble our ears. Once when I was driving, he chomped down on my right earlobe with the full force of his beak, drawing blood! I knocked him off my shoulder, whereupon he retreated to Helen's shoulder and pointedly ignored me for the remainder of the day, pouting. When he was young, and before he could fly well, Benjamin greatly enjoyed walks, sitting on a shoulder. At dusk, he always grew somewhat frantic, looking for a high safe perch on which to spend the night. We found that if we could somehow get through about half an hour of frantic unrest, once it got dark, Ben would settle down for the night inside the car. Occasionally, we did allow him to fly up and roost overnight in a tree outside the car. Ben was very good about flying back down to us the next day, when he would alight on a head or finger. He was a great bird.

We had had Benjamin for only several months when tragedy fell. One moonlit summer night, we allowed him to perch high in a gum tree. In the dark of the night, we awoke to hear him squawk, followed by the fluttering of his wings and a short croak. We jumped up

*Benjamin
the cockatoo*

immediately and looked all over for him, calling out his name in the dark, but he didn't appear. In the early morning light, we determined from tracks that a fox had walked underneath the tree, spooked Ben, who foolishly flew down to the ground, whereupon he was pounced upon, carried away, and eaten. All we found were a few pink and gray feathers. The loss of Benjamin left us in mourning, with a great and painful void for a long time.

Two unusual birds nest in the arid interior of Western Australia: these are the Spotted Bowerbird and the Malleefowl. In both species, males have dispensed with gaudy plumage and have substituted structures to court females. The bower of a male bowerbird is a carefully constructed tube of grass almost a meter long, open at the top. At each end, the male places an assortment of colored objects. Females are led back and forth through the tube and are shown the collections. The male with the most impressive bower wins the females. Malleefowl males build enormous mounds of decaying vegetation and heat-retaining earth, the heat of decomposition assisting incubation. One of these I saw was made of ironstone gravel and must have weighed many tons and required thousands upon thousands of hours, probably numerous generations, to build—it was about five meters in diameter and a full meter high with a flat top! After using these to attract a willing female, they are used as incubators. Malleefowl do not sit on their eggs, but bury them deep inside these specially built, heat-retentive "nests."

Excellent firewood abounds in most of the southern half of the desert interior of Western Australia. One seldom has to walk more than a dozen meters to gather ample fuel for a roaring evening campfire. Dead mulga trees are everywhere in hard country. (Mulga limbs never seem to break where you want or expect them to, and one often gets cut and injured while gathering and breaking mulga branches.) Mulga wood is exceedingly hard and burns both clean and long, although it does not have enough volatiles to give off flame for very long—mulga coals are too hot for baked potatoes, but they usually last until morning, making it easy to restart the fire to boil the billy. In sandy country, dead marble gum branches are the best firewood—they don't burn as hot or as long as mulga, but gum fires flame for longer and burn at a lower temperature, which is better for cooking.

Most of Australia is fairly flat. Precipitation is scant and exceedingly variable, but sometimes falls in massive amounts. When a heavy rain finally does arrive, runoff is limited by the restricted topographic relief, causing low-lying areas to become shallow lakes. Such places quickly turn into treacherous bogs, which can stay that way for a long while afterward, even after the surface dries out again. In such a situation, one can pull off the track to camp for the night, with everything looking just fine, and then awake in the morning only to find that the car has broken through the thin dry surface crust and sunk down in underlying mud up to its floorboards! Many tracks are cut below the surface and thus become impassable during "the wet." Frequently, there are detours around the lowest spots with rough signs marked In the Wet. Drainage ditches cut in along the edges of roads become mud traps. Nothing is much more pathetic than a sturdy four-wheel drive helplessly mired up to its axles in bottomless mud, like a dead elephant.

The first few times this happens, you think that you'll never be able to get out. We always seemed to get bogged in really remote places where one could wait for months before anyone else might happen along. One of our most memorable "bogs" was near the dry lakebed of Lake Eyre, in the driest part of Australia. We were out in this remote, uninhabited area looking for a rare snakelike legless pygopodid lizard that at the time was known from only a single specimen, the type specimen in the National Museum, which had been collected during the late 1800s. Someone had speculated that the genus *Ophidiocephalus* might have since gone extinct, but it seemed more likely that no one had been able to find its habitat (in fact, it was later rediscovered). I hoped that we might get lucky and refind it.

On an overcast day, we drove down an abandoned old track in South Australia to the location given as the type locality, Charlotte Waters, an abandoned telegraph station. These were only ruins in an exceedingly bleak place, and we found no lizards there, but continued driving south and eastward looking for suitable habitat. Low cloud cover was continuous that day, and it finally began to rain, just a sprinkle at first, but then the rain turned to a steady drizzle. When it began to pour, serious mud quickly began to form. Hoping to reach higher ground, I kept following the track, but it led instead to even lower ground. Soon I was plowing great deep furrows through the mud and slipping out of control all over the "track." After just barely making it through a couple of very muddy low spots, I felt that I couldn't turn back safely. But conditions just got steadily worse and worse, with the track descending right into an open muddy lakebed (normally dry). Suddenly, I found myself sliding completely off the track, miring in deeply to the axle on the left side (it really is a "sinking" feeling!). At that time, I was inexperienced at driving in mud and equally naïve about how to extract a vehicle from it. Doing all the wrong things that rainy afternoon, such as spinning the wheels and digging, merely dug us in deeper and deeper. By nightfall, we were really mired in to stay. And it continued to rain the entire time.

We spent that night extremely disillusioned trying to sleep inside the Land Rover, which was pitched uncomfortably at a sharp angle. Rain continued throughout the night. During a fitful and relatively sleepless night, we had nightmares of the entire dry lake filling up with meters of water and bottomless mud. It was frightening, to say the least. A little before dawn the rain finally stopped. Once the sun came out, much of the standing surface water quickly evaporated. Both of us worked most of the next day to get Mat out and rolling again. First, we unloaded everything heavy. Then, using our precious wallaby jack, I raised one wheel at a time as high as possible. Helen and I carried thousands of rocks down from a small hill nearby. Trip after trip, we poured the rocks into the gaping mudholes beneath the tires. When no more rocks would fit, I dropped the wheel down, and it pushed the rocks down into the soft, squishy mud. We repeated this process ad nauseam. We also built many meters of rocky road in front of the vehicle to help get her up and going again. If you rush it, you're likely just to get rebogged. Both of us were exhausted and covered with mud when, hours later, I finally climbed into the empty vehicle and said, "Well, here goes nothing." After a fearful, shaky start, I got her moving down our little rocky road, got the revs up, and got her

Matilda, bogged down in the washed-out remains of a "road" (central Australia, 1966)

rolling up to the top of the hill from which we had been gathering rocks all day. Slogging through the mud, we then had to carry everything up the hill and reload. It was a traumatic experience, but not the first or the last time we got bogged, either.

Since then, I have of necessity gained considerable experience extracting vehicles from bogs (more than I would like!). To avoid getting bogged, one should always try to steer away from the edge of the track (this, however, is not easy, since a vehicle slides on the slippery mud and gets pulled sideways toward and into the softer shoulders of deep mud). Don't try to drive around puddles if this means you have to drive on the edge of the track—the hard-packed wheel ruts in the center of the track are usually safer than the unpacked edges. Once bogged, do not simply put it in low range and spin the wheels, as this will just dig the car in deeper and deeper. Even if you have a strong winch, the first thing to do is to unload the vehicle—it's hard enough to get its own weight out, let alone a massive payload. Carry the contents forward to high, dry ground where you will reload them after getting out. One side is often deeply mired, whereas the other side still remains on fairly firm ground. If so, do not try to dig on the mired side, but get out your high-lift jack, and some sort of large block, and lift the stuck tires, one by one, up as high as possible. Fill in underneath them with rocks, if possible (otherwise, use sticks and logs). Then, drop the car down, and repeat.

If you can really get into the spirit, you won't even mind being covered with slime from head to toe! With any luck, each cycle will bring the car up a little more (sometimes, in a truly bottomless bog, one doesn't gain much elevation until a considerable volume of solid material has been placed beneath the wheel!). If you're prepared to work at it, it is possible to get out of almost any bog, although you often feel it's hopeless.

Another hazard of driving in the Australian bush is flat tires (called "punctures" down under). These are particularly frequent when you must drive across country through mulga scrub. Sharp mulga snags sticking up in grass are hard to see. A tire "staked" in the sidewall is ruined. Several flat tires in a row on a single trip can constitute a serious problem, since it is not easy to repair one without hydraulic tools. Sometimes, you can break a tire off the rim by driving over it with the car (be sure to do this while you still have four good tires). After a time, a wily old Aussie bushman shared with me the secret of the problem, and its obvious solution: On the first pass cross-country, tires knock snags forward in the direction of travel. On the return trip, tires gouge into these sharp snags "set" by the first pass from the opposite direction. Therefore, never follow your own tire ruts in the reverse direction to which they were made. Always drive back a different route or straddle the one you came in on.

We soon came to appreciate the full meaning of the Australian slang terms "bush happy," and "too long in the bush." These refer to the state of mind one reaches after having been away from civilization for too long. One begins to lose all the amenities of proper behavior. To be a desert rat, you must take water conservation *very* seriously[1] and be able to go for a week or two without bathing. You also have to be able to tolerate your own body odors as well as those of your companions. (I'll never forget one excellent assistant, whose un-washed feet smelled like strong limburger cheese and who insisted on removing his boots as we drove between study sites!) In the desert, I can wash my hair *and* take a bath in less than a gallon of water. Upon return to civilization, a real shower or bath is such a pleasant luxury, although I am always a little surprised at how much of my "tan" washes off, not to mention great flakes of skin! When you really get bushed, it takes a week or two before you can face the prospect of returning to the outback again. People who live way out on isolated stations are said to go "tropo" (for "tropical"?) when they become a little crazed due to the lack of contact with humanity.

When winter came and lizarding got slow, we decided to take a trip up to the warmer tropics. I had always wanted to cross the "dead heart" of central Australia, but so far we had merely skirted the edges and made limited forays out into it. Obtaining permission to travel through the large central Aboriginal reserves, we topped up fuel and water in Laverton and set out for Alice Springs, via Warburton. A road sign said Caution: No Fuel or Water for 570 km—Obtain Supplies in Laverton. Grinding along on this little-used track, Matilda suddenly died, stopped dead in her tracks with both tanks full of fuel. High school auto shop to the rescue: (1) Check carburetor to see if the engine is getting gas, yes. (2) Check to see if a spark is reaching the plugs, no. (3) Look around to determine why not . . . notice that the throttle linkage has been rubbing against the main ignition cable from the coil to the distributor, has worn through the insulation, and the spark is grounding out before reaching the distributor. Solution: wrap ignition cable in electrical insulating tape, and secure it away from the throttle linkage apparatus. Five minutes later we're on our way again, just a little scare, ha ha. (I carried a spare fuel pump and many other spare parts, just in case they were needed, of course.)

A couple of days later, at Warburton, we topped up with fuel and water again and set out on the truly uninhabited portion of the long journey. Out in the "dead centre" you find yourself several hundred kilometers from anyone in any direction! The Schwerin Mural Crescent region, just a little north of the three-way border between Western Australia, South Australia, and the Northern Territory, is spectacularly beautiful desert-mountain range country. It was an eerie feeling to be so remote, driving on tracks that no one had been on in months! Around the central mountains, the track was so badly washed out that we couldn't follow it and had to detour cross-country alongside it (this was very slow going). We had been told that one could sometimes find stockpiles of abandoned fuel in drums along-side tracks out in the center, but one could not rely on finding such free fuel. Accordingly, I had refilled every container I had up to the brim at the last source of petrol in Warburton. When we came upon literally dozens of fifty-gallon drums of aviation petrol (used because its high octane rating keeps it usable longer), I could only make room for about twenty-five to thirty gallons. It was with real dismay that I left behind many hundreds of gallons of the precious liquid gold!

At one point near Wingelena, a mining company helicopter flying overhead landed, and two guys got out wondering what we were doing out in the middle of nowhere, where were we going, were we all right, etc. Finally, weeks later, we came out the other side in the Northern Territory at the Aboriginal settlement of Papunya.

On the way back from Darwin, we passed by a butcher shop with great cuts of cheap beef in the window. Being starved for red meat, we bought two huge T-bone steaks for the unbelievable price of A$1.75 (only 72 cents a pound!). Our mouths drooled the rest of the day at the mere thought of what a scrumptious dinner we'd enjoy that night. We found an exquisite campsite along the Victoria River, and it seemed that it would be a perfect evening. With an idyllic background of graceful gum trees silhouetted against a fiery-red sunset reflected in the water, we built up a bank of hard dead *Eucalyptus* firewood and started it burning. Borrowing the grill off Matilda's radiator for a cooking grill, we broiled our steaks to perfection over ideal coals, salivating all the while. But when we tried to eat them, we were at first appalled, and then amused—the steaks were as tough as leather, virtually inedible (this was our first and last attempt to ingest the

wild range beef of the Northern Territory). We did manage to eat most of the tenderloins, though it took some serious chewing. Aussies must know some secret way to tenderize and cook that stuff to make it more edible!

A sign like this could save your life.

Returning in 1978 as a Guggenheim Fellow with a research grant from the National Geographic Society that included a fully equipped Toyota Land Cruiser (I named this one "Old Lady"), I was pleased to find the Eyre Highway paved (a new sealed road had also been built for mining purposes from Leonora to Laverton, making my life considerably easier). However, I was dismayed to see all the road-killed emus, wombats, and "roos" along these high-speed roads. Buses and trucks, especially, just mow these creatures down. Kangaroos and emus are frequently slow to take fright, and when they do move, they often run right into the path of the vehicle swerving to miss them. "Roo bars," heavy-duty bumper bars, are essential on vehicles in rural Australia. The many corpses, however, do feed crows and ravens as well as the magnificent wedge-tailed eagle (reminiscent of the North American golden eagle), which fill the empty vulture niche in Australia.

Abandoned
homestead near
Lake Yeo

Late in 1978, I crossed the Great Sandy and Gibson deserts, a total distance of well over a thousand kilometers, without meeting or seeing anyone. Because I was completely alone for over two weeks in such a remote area, this was perhaps the eeriest journey I have ever undertaken in central Australia. Not long after I crossed the point of no return, it began to rain and rained all night. I had nightmares of the tracks ahead turning into bogs and did, in fact, get mired in for most of a day.

Several times I have come across recently abandoned homesteads in remote outback regions. An immense investment and a great deal of effort go into putting together a viable station, with its many buildings and accessories: homes with fly-screened verandas, garages, bunkhouses, shops, shearing sheds, outstations, paddocks, corrals, fences, gates, cattleguards, wells, tanks, windmills, and radio-transmitting antennae. Fees must also be paid to the government land department for the pastoral lease. In the best of times, it is a marginal existence on most Australian stations, and when droughts are prolonged, all stock can be lost. Wandering around such a place of dashed hopes, you really feel for some tough, determined bloke and

THE LIZARD MAN SPEAKS

his tough wife, who put everything they had, both financially and physically, into the project for many years in the hope of making it pay. When children's toys are scattered about the grounds, and women's magazines are blowing in the wind, it is truly heart-breaking.

At the conclusion of my year-long Fulbright scholarship down under in 1991, most of which was spent doing fieldwork in Western Australia, I went on a sort of "whistle-stop" seminar tour of eastern universities. While I was arranging my schedule from a Post Office box address in Kalgoorlie, one of my eastern hosts commented, "I hope you are enjoying Kalgoorlie—a town with an interesting reputation." Kalgoorlie is a mining town, with a strongly male-biased sex ratio. Pubs have a tradition termed "skimpy," which involves a scantily-clad bar maid parading around serving drinks while male drinkers ogle. Outside the pubs, chalkboards announce who's going to go skimpy tonight. Brothels are legal in Kalgoorlie, although the words "prostitutes" and "prostitution" are never used. One brothel sported doors painted bright red, with sexy-sounding names like "Angela" and "Brigette" painted on them in white. Another, called "Ring my Bell," posted a blackboard with all the present girls' names. Reason dictated that I not be tempted to partake of such pleasures of the flesh (having made it to a fairly ripe old age without yet acquiring an incurable social disease, it would hardly be sensible to risk it all at this late date).

NOTE TO CHAPTER 2

1. Due to its weight and limited availability, every drop of water must be reused until it is scummy. Water used to wash your face and hands is still suitable for evaporative cooling or for washing your feet. Indeed, I think in terms of "flushing" the sink when the water contained therein begins to get really ripe!

LIZARDING

Three

~ • • • • • ~

I ENJOY "LIZARDING" AS MUCH OR MORE THAN MANY PEOPLE relish fishing. Indeed, there are actually quite a few similarities between the two activities, which I suspect satisfy our primitive hunter-gatherer instincts. In both cases, some skill is required in pitting one's wits against those of a fast, agile small animal. Lizards are simply spectacularly beautiful terrestrial fish. I haven't yet attempted to catch lizards with a hook and line, though that might actually be possible (they sometimes lunge open-mouthed at a nylon noose dangled near their heads when you're trying to snare them). Instead, I catch lizards live by grabbing them by hand or by noosing them with a fishing rod and a tiny nylon snare around their neck. Some species are slow enough that individuals can simply be picked up without any particular skill being required. Catching an alert fast lizard by grabbing it requires extreme speed, commitment, and coordination, as well as some cunning in the approach. For much of my research, it is essential that I collect the animal for a permanent museum specimen, dead or alive, in any way possible, so I often shoot lizards with either a BB gun or .22-caliber dust shot.

Finding lizards in the North American deserts was fairly simple and straightforward. As one walks quietly along, most species are readily encountered and observed. A couple of arboreal species require somewhat more careful scrutiny. To quantify relative abundance of lizards in the U.S. deserts, I wore a pedometer calibrated to my stride and tallied up all the lizards we sighted, species by species, as my assistants and I took long lizard "treks" across the desert each morning. At night, we walked across the desert carrying a bright Coleman lantern, finding nocturnal geckos and snakes by their body shine. Lizards were collected, individually tagged, weighed, and measured, and preserved for later analysis of their reproductive condition and stomach contents back in the laboratory (these specimens are now safely ensconced in museums—many of the study areas they came from have since been destroyed by agriculture and/or encroaching urbanization, so these specimens constitute the only record of what was once present before the onslaught of humans).

Locating most species of lizards in Australia proved to be rather more difficult and required developing some expertise in stalking and tracking. One has to work hard to find and to collect most species of lizards in Australia. I have frequently worked all day long for ten specimens, sometimes even fewer. Guns proved to be relatively useless with many wary skinks, because these lizards are constantly moving, and often out of sight, so we had to develop new collecting techniques such as "whomping," a term we developed for flattening spinifex tussocks with the broad side of a shovel. If the lizard darts out, you whomp the tussock it runs to, etc. Sometimes a lizard is squashed flat, but very often a nearly perfect specimen results. This works well enough if you really put your back into it, although both Helen and I ended up injuring our lower backs in this manner. At times, we were so stiff that we could barely bend over. We had to do a lot of digging for lizards, too. After a whomp, if no lizard appears in the spinifex, one must dig out the burrow systems underneath the tussock (frequently, however, the skink then darts out again and escapes). Sometimes you get a lizard you didn't even bargain for!

Other species of lizards could only be collected by digging them up in their burrows. We moved truckloads of sand, and literally wore out shovels in such activities, which also took their toll on our overworked backs. A large nocturnal skink, *Egernia striata*, one of the few skinks that has evolved elliptical pupils, digs elaborate tunnel systems that are used as retreats by many other species of reptiles, both diurnal and nocturnal. These complex burrows are an important feature of the Australian sandy deserts, with several interconnected openings often as far as a meter apart, and up to half a meter deep, vaguely reminiscent of a tiny rabbit warren. Most of the sand removed from a *striata* burrow is piled up in a large mound outside one "main" entrance. We excavated hundreds of these burrows. The

Eric and François attempt to catch a wily skink in the spinifex.

best procedure is to cover all but one entrance, and dig a steep-sided pit for that entrance; then, attack each of the other entrances, always keeping pits clean and too steep for a lizard to climb out. Be ready to pounce! It is rather disillusioning to lose a lizard after spending three-quarters of an hour working up a sweat moving a large wheelbarrow-load of sand. It is always wise to check all such pits the next day, as sometimes other lizards appear in them (this is how we collected our first small marsupial mouse, an undescribed genus in 1967, now named *Ningaui*). You must remain ever cautious when digging out burrows, for sometimes they contain large venomous elapid snakes!

Another smaller and more crepuscular *Egernia* species, *E. inornata*, digs a much simpler shallow burrow, consisting of a U-shaped tube with but one arm of the "U" open (this is the sole entrance and only open exit to the burrow); the other arm of the "U" typically stops just below the surface of the ground and is used as an escape hatch by breaking through the sand's crust in an emergency. *E. inornata* individuals often have two such burrows ten to twenty meters apart.

The procedure for digging these out is to first locate the escape hatch by scraping off the surface sand around the main open entrance, then put a deep pile of sand over it and excavate using the deep, clean pit method described above.

Finding geckos at night by their dim eyeshine is tricky. You have to be looking from just the right distance away. Too close or too far, and you simply cannot see geckos. Spiders and certain insects also have bright sparkling eyeshine, and since these are plentiful, one must learn to ignore them but perceive and distinguish the much fainter eyeshine of geckos. Helen proved to be an excellent geckoer; night after night, she would return with two to three times as many as I could. She enjoyed geckoing, likening it to an "Easter egg hunt." This analogy was based both on their beauty and the fact that geckos are easily picked up. In contrast to diurnal lizards, many geckos are relatively easy to capture once they have been located. Luckily, several of my other assistants also developed good skill at finding geckos by eyeshine. One clever field assistant, Bill Giles, invented a useful method to catch speedy, wary nocturnal arboreal geckos that stay on the other side of marble gum tree trunks. Bill's "shovel trick" is simple and efficient: one simply holds a shovel in the left hand, and, with the right, grabbing hand free, poised, and ready, sticks the broad side of the shovel around the backside of the tree trunk and moves it up or down—very frequently, the gecko darts around into the light where it can be grabbed.

One of the hazards of geckoing is getting lost—it is very easy to lose your bearings at night, and I have had several close calls when it looked as if I would have to spend the entire night out (it can get quite cold in the desert at night!). After a time, I started to leave a light shining at camp to help find our way back, but even this failed when one got a little too far away or the bulb burned out or the wind blew the light over. Finally, I constructed a proper fail-safe twelve-volt "beacon" with dual red and green lights that could be clamped high up on a tree or radio antenna fitted with long leads to reach the car battery.

Burning a large clump of spinifex is another way to obtain some species of lizards that are exceedingly difficult to collect because they seldom leave these tussocks. The spinifex-dwelling gecko *Diplodactylus elderi* is difficult to collect in any other way, as it is seldom found even with eyeshine. A cryptic skink called *Cyclodomorphus melanops* is a similar denizen of large spinifex tussocks, as are the flapfoot legless

Delma (pygopodid lizards). However, because burning always makes me nervous that a fire might escape and set fire to the whole desert, I burn spinifex only when winds are relatively calm (which is infrequent in the desert). One must stay by the burning spinifex with a shovel, ready to pounce or shoot. Moreover, it is wise to scrape away the ashes and dig up the burrows beneath the tussock after burning; occasionally, one finds a dead lizard that has been killed by the heat.

In my old age, I have recently come to rely on a more passive, but powerful, technique to capture many kinds of lizards: pit trapping with drift fences. One sinks five-gallon plastic buckets into the sand, their tops flush with the surface, and erects short little screen fences to divert lizards into the resulting pit traps. At a reasonably good site, each such trap in an arrangement will yield a lizard about every fourth or fifth day. With dozens of traps, a fair sample can be captured each day. Such a trapline is expensive and time-consuming to set up, requires regular checking, and lids must be secured on the traps when not in use (I also put in a rough stick diagonally so that if the top is removed, most animals can still climb out). Fences require some maintenance, as they are damaged and destroyed by animals as well as by the elements. Animals occasionally try to eat the fence, and kangaroos regularly punch holes in drift fences with their toes when hopping cross-country. Foxes and dingoes pull up fences and sometimes pull the lids off traps.

Ants are extremely plentiful in Australia, and they frequently mass at a pit trap. A swarm of ants can completely dismember a small lizard and carry it away in pieces within a few hours! Other lizard predators, including foxes, monitor lizards (*Varanus*), and certain birds, learn to raid traps. A major advantage of the pit-trap technique is that live lizards are captured undamaged; disadvantages are that no data are collected on precise time of activity, body temperatures, microhabitats, etc. Use of this technique also ties you to one spot and requires constant checking of traps (in hot weather, trap deaths can occur within an hour, meaning that you must check traps frequently during the most unpleasant time of the day when they are usually empty). Rare and uncommon species that are exceedingly difficult to capture in other ways often do fall into pit traps. Trapping success can be expressed in lizards per trap day, facilitating comparisons of relative abundances between sites because the common method of collection provides a sort of standard unit of measurement. Certain species are adept at avoiding pit traps and must still be collected in other ways.

During four years of wandering around in the Australian deserts, a number of events happened but once. Fresh in my mind's eye, I only wish that I had been able to capture them on film. One wonders, if one could wander forty years or four hundred or four thousand, what amazing sights one would see! One of my fantasies is to be able to stand at one spot for a century to make an accurate estimate of what ecologists term "point diversity." I am convinced that over such a long time period, one would see all the species present at that site wander past that particular point. Over a long enough period of time, one might also witness invasions of new species and extinctions of existing species.

One such once-in-a-lifetime event occurred when a small individual of the large monitor species *Varanus gouldi* attempted to subdue and eat a large individual of the pygmy monitor species *Varanus gilleni*. It was truly an epic battle, two varanids about the same size, tails entwined, rolling over and over in the dust! The *gouldi* had the *gilleni* by the nape of its neck, and the *gilleni* was wrapped around the *gouldi*, struggling to free itself. Helen and I came upon this prehistoric scene while driving slowly down the track deep in the Great Victoria Desert. I had collated all the museum locality data for desert *Varanus* for papers I intended to write, and I was acutely aware that *V. gilleni* was known only from a handful of localities in central Western Australia. This was the first one that I had ever seen in the wild. At that point in time, no *Varanus gilleni* had ever been collected from the Great Victoria Desert—this would be about a 400–500-km extension of the known geographic range. Thus, it was quite important to collect the specimen as a voucher specimen and a permanent record. However, the fighting monitors were also a sight of a lifetime that I very much wanted to preserve on film. As Helen kept her eyes on the two struggling lizards, I tried frantically to dig out the telephoto lens and get it onto the camera. (Monitors usually run from humans on foot but will sometimes hold their ground before a vehicle.) Before I could get the lens and camera ready, she shouted, "There they go," and jumped out to follow them. I ran after, wringing my hands at losing both the picture and the rare specimen! Luckily, however, the *gouldi* released the *gilleni*, and Helen managed to save the day when she came upon the stunned *gilleni*, quickly stepped on it, and then grabbed it. After we photographed this beautiful maroon-and-gold lizard, it became the first validated and permanent record of that species from that part of Western Australia (a dozen years later, I managed to collect a second *gilleni* about 200 km to the west of this locality).

We had traveled over 12,000 kilometers without finding a single thorny devil, the agamid that has converged on North American horned lizards, which belong to a different family. Studying this species to compare it with its ecological equivalent was one of my primary objectives in coming to Australia. Just as I was beginning to despair that we would never be able to find a *Moloch*, one day there was one crossing the road. Like a horned lizard, the lizard didn't move and was easily captured. Immediately, we took it to some soft sand and backed off a ways, allowing it to walk and leave a trail. We studied its track with care and eventually learned how to find these elusive lizards by following their delicate footprints. This is far from easy, and even now I often cannot locate individuals of this species. Tracks that lead into a large bush or a messy area of litter and bushes cannot be followed, and one must try to find the animal by sight.

Once, on a very remote site deep in the desert where *Moloch* had never before been recorded, we had spent most of the day trying to find an animal whose track went around and around in a large figure eight. We were running out of food and water and had to return to civilization the next day. It was getting late in the day, and the sun would soon set. Helen and I were standing a couple of meters apart at the center of the figure eight, shaking our heads, wondering where the *Moloch* was, when suddenly both of us saw it at the same time, hunkered down right between us. Needless to say, these animals are exceedingly well camouflaged and very difficult to see, even when you have the correct search image!

Sands constitute a natural event recorder, leaving a record of what creatures have moved past. Strong winds regularly dull and erase all tracks. Although it took a good while, both Helen and I eventually trained ourselves to become fairly skilled at reading the record in the sand. Tracks are difficult to see during midday when the sun is high or on overcast days. Morning and afternoon are prime times for tracking, when the sun is low in the sky and shadows are long. We learned that tracks are best seen by looking into the light. After a bit of experience, we began to be able to judge the "run" of the track, that is, where the animal is headed. It is almost like becoming the lizard yourself. This allows one to move ahead quickly, cutting the track at intervals, to find the lizard rapidly. You can even tell the approximate age of a track by its crispness and whether or not other tracks, say

those of nocturnal species, cross over the track in question. Nothing is much more exciting than finding a crisp new track less than an hour old, for you know that the maker of that track is close by at the end of the track. It is like finding a line guaranteed to lead you to a neat lizard! On a very hot trail I always walk as quietly as possible, barely breathing, scouting ahead to look for the lizard itself. Tracking large lizards across sandy areas has become one of my favorite pastimes. One can learn a great deal about wary, unobservable species such as *Varanus* in this way. It is an incredible thrill when the track suddenly becomes the magnificent animal, captured in midstride, frozen in time. More often than not, however, before you see it, the animal breaks into a run and dives down a hole or climbs up a tree and escapes into a hollow. The track of a running animal is often harder to follow than that of one walking.

My first experiences with tracking were more than a little frustrating, as the animals I was following made large loops with the track frequently coming back to the point of origin. Being relatively unskilled, I couldn't determine for certain exactly where the track began. I had followed many sets of one such very distinctive type of track without ever finding the animal, but was not about to give up

Helen contemplates the insurmountable task of trying to extract a lizard from a mammoth spini tussock.

Lizarding   57

until I discovered the identity of this mysterious beast that left a bold broad tail mark. It could either be a large skink or a monitor lizard. One day, I followed such a fresh track to a fallen, burned-out, hollow dead *Eucalyptus* branch. The track went directly up to the hollow end of this small log, but no exiting track was evident. Carefully circling around and around, I determined that, indeed, the lizard had not departed. I picked up the log and peered in but couldn't see very far because of the curvature of the log. So I plugged the ends with other smaller logs and carried my "surprise package" back to camp. Breaking the log apart, I found a large jet-black racehorse monitor lizard, *Varanus tristis*, previously unknown from the deserts! (These cryptic lizards turned out to be ubiquitous on all my study sites throughout the Great Victoria Desert.)

During my first year in Australia, with a great deal of effort and hard work, I managed to capture about twenty *Varanus tristis*. On a second trip, arriving back at camp after a day's absence to pick up a fresh, new field assistant, Bill Giles, I noted a very fresh *tristis* track crossing right through camp. To introduce Bill to the art of tracking, we followed it. Instead of going from tree to tree, this animal headed out into a large treeless "meadow" of spinifex. Fifteen minutes, and about half a kilometer later, just as the sun was setting, I lost the track. As I circled around and around looking for it in dismay (time was rapidly running out!), Bill said, "Hey, Eric, what's this?" pointing to the tip of a black tail sticking out of a clump of spinifex. Immediately, I pounced on it and showed him his first *Varanus tristis*, telling him how hard it was to get these animals and that we were extremely fortunate this time and not to expect a repeat. Bill's response was that during the time he was with me, we would set a quota and get "a *tristis* a day," a feat much easier said than done. I did not think it remotely possible. However, during the next six weeks, we worked extremely hard tracking down these evasive lizards, and then, with the help of a bow saw, nylon rope, and the car, pulled down dead trees and chopped the lizards out of hollow logs. Some days we got two, other days none, but when all was said and done, we had indeed collected a *tristis* a day! As we worked at this task, we thought up a neat plot for a novel or a movie, "the *tristis* hunters," which would center around survival in the desert by eating lizards following a nuclear holocaust.

Bill and I each carried a small specially designed military signaling mirror tied on nylon straps around our necks. These mirrors are designed so that one can see through them exactly where a beam is being reflected. Sending a flash of sunlight is a useful way to catch someone's attention silently from far away. Mirrors are also extremely useful for sending light into dark holes and hollows of logs and trees. You can hold the mirror in the shade, or even down in the bottom of a pit where you couldn't possibly get your head, and actually look sideways into a burrow. With two people, one can "divert" sunlight virtually anywhere, and bright light can be shone wherever needed. "Give me some light here, would you?" One can even peer into a dark burrow way down in the bottom of a deep pit in this way!

Australian *Varanus* are exceedingly wary, essentially unapproachable and unobservable lizards. Fortunately, however, they leave fairly conspicuous tracks, and one may deduce quite a lot about their biology from careful study of this spoor. The largest species, the perentie *V. giganteus*, reaches two meters or more in total length, whereas some of the smaller "pygmy goannas," such as the ubiquitous and very important lizard predator *V. eremius*, achieve lengths of only about forty centimeters. Two other species, *V. gouldi* and *V. tristis*, are intermediate in size. Individuals of all four of these species range over extensive areas and consume very large prey items, particularly other vertebrates (especially lizards). *V. tristis*, and two other little-known small species, *V. caudolineatus* and *V. gilleni*, are climbers, whereas the other three species (*V. eremius*, *V. gouldi*, and *V. giganteus*) are terrestrial. Still another very tiny species, *V. brevicauda*, is also terrestrial. Up to six species of these monitor lizards can be found together on the same study area. Each species leaves its own distinct track. Daily forays typically cover a distance of a kilometer. *V. gouldi* captures most of its prey (predominantly lizards and reptile eggs) by digging; it appears to have a very keen sense of smell, using its long, forked, very snake-like tongue extensively.

V. tristis also consumes other lizards as well as baby birds (and probably bird eggs); its very distinctive track typically runs more or less directly from tree to tree (these monitors climb most of these trees looking for food). *V. tristis* activity is highly seasonal, and the animals rely on building up fat reserves during times of plenty to get them through lean periods. Once, camped on a study site where I had never seen a *tristis* track in many weeks of work over several months in the midst of a prolonged drought, I noticed a beady black eye peering out of a small black hole in a burned-out *Eucalyptus* tree—chopping the hollow tree open revealed an extremely emaciated *Varanus tristis*, literally skin and bones, waiting for the drought to break!

Hearing a Galah Cockatoo screeching loudly as if in distress nearby first caught my attention. The bird was on the ground when first sighted, with its crest held high and wings partially outstretched. The Galah flew up onto a fallen log under a marble gum tree and then into the tree, which proved to be its nesting tree. A large *V. tristis* clambered over the same log toward the tree. The cockatoo continued to screech and then began to harass the lizard. When the lizard climbed about three meters up the tree and went around out of sight on the other side, the Galah attacked and actually drove the monitor back down the tree. The Galah's mate was also present. These large climbing predatory lizards must constitute a potent threat to hole-nesting parrots (I have found baby birds in their stomachs).

Varanus eremius are fairly common in Australian sandy deserts, judging from the frequency of their unique, conspicuous tracks. Unlike the larger goannas, they are active all year long. However, this beautiful little red *Varanus* is extremely wary and very seldom seen. Nevertheless, a great deal about its activities can be inferred from its tracks. Statements to follow are based upon impressions I have gained while following literally hundreds of kilometers of *eremius* tracks on foot. Individuals usually cover great distances when foraging. I have often followed a fresh track for distances of up to a kilometer. Tracks indicate little tendency to stay within a delimited area; home ranges of these lizards must be extremely large. These pygmy monitors are attracted to fresh holes and will often visit any digging of human origin within a few days after it is made. In contrast to *V. gouldi*, *V. eremius* do not dig for their prey, but rather rely upon catching it above ground. More than once, I have noted an *eremius* track intercept the track of another smaller lizard with evidence of an ensuing tussle. One such pair of tracks came together, rolled down the side of a sandridge leaving a trail of big and little tail lash marks, and finally became one track, dragging away a fat belly.

Once, as she was stalking a small skink, Helen actually observed an *eremius* attack another lizard from ambush. On this occasion, a large *eremius* jumped out of a loose *Triodia* tussock when a small blue-tailed skink (*Ctenotus calurus*) came within a few centimeters of the edge of the tussock. Stomach contents reveal that over 70 percent of the *eremius* diet by volume consists of other lizards, whereas large grasshoppers plus an occasional large cockroach or scorpion constitute most of the remainder. Nearly any other lizard species small enough to be subdued is eaten (sixty stomachs with food contained forty-two individual lizard prey representing some fourteen other species in addition to other items). In a typical foraging run, an individual *eremius* often visits, and goes down into, several burrows belonging to other lizard species, especially the complex burrow systems of *Egernia striata* mentioned above. These activities could be in search of prey, related to thermoregulatory activities, or simply involved with escape responses. Certainly an *eremius* remembers the exact positions of the burrows it has visited, since it almost inevitably runs directly to the nearest one when confronted with the emergency of a lizard collector.

The pygmy monitor lizard *Varanus eremius* is my favorite lizard: like me, it is a lizard hunter. During the mid-1970s, our Botany and Zoology graduate students in population biology founded an arcane club they called the "Darwinian Fitness Club." Customized green T-shirts were made up with the name of the club on the front side, while that particular person's favorite study organism's scientific name was on the back side. On the eve of my departure for the deserts of Western Australia for a year's sabbatical as a Guggenheim Fellow, these graduate students held a going-away party and made me an honorary member of their club (the first faculty member to be so honored, presumably because I was a proven "field man"). They presented me with my own customized T-shirt sporting "*Varanus eremius*" on the back side. I wore this T-shirt with pride down under. Aussies puzzled over it, thinking that it was odd for someone rather out of shape to proclaim publicly to be some kind of a physical fitness buff (of course, Darwinian fitness is simply relative reproductive success).

By far the most impressive desert lizard in Australia is the enormous perentie, *Varanus giganteus*, which attains a total length of more than two meters. Highly prized as food, and hence sought after by Aborigines, these large mammal-like predators have evolved mam-

Eric, sporting his "Darwinian Fitness Club" T-shirt, gets bitten by his favorite species of lizard, Varanus eremius *(Red Sands, 1978).*

malian-level intelligence. Once, I found a perentie track that inter-cepted my own track, then turned back on itself, suggesting these lizards possess incredible olfactory sensitivity as well as acute intelli-gence. They are exceedingly unapproachable. Their food must once have been small wallabies and mid-sized marsupials, many of which are now extinct. Nowadays, perenties feed largely on introduced European rabbits (we flushed the stomach of one and found that it had eaten another monitor lizard, a *Varanus gouldi*). I wanted very much to see, and to photograph, a perentie during my stay down under, but couldn't seem to find one. Talking with a station owner one day, I was told that just a few weeks before his dogs had one at bay, which he had killed down in the south paddock very close to one of my study areas. When I asked, "Why did you kill it?" his response was that perenties were simply "vermin." I insisted that he take me to the spot, and I took the battered head to try to make some sort of a skull for a specimen. Its long, serrated, sharp cutting teeth were most impressive!

Many species of lizards occur on rocky areas that are not present in the sandy desert. Outcrops are known as "tors" in Australia. I wanted to become familiar with as many different species of lizards as possible. On our last bush trip of the first expedition down under, Helen and I therefore decided to do some incidental collecting on such a rocky area with granitic outcrops. We ate our standard lunch of Vitawheat crackers and cheddar cheese with Vegemite, washed down with a cool drink, sitting in Matilda away from the bush flies (I had fitted screens to some of the windows). After a quiet lunch, I got out to take a whiz, walking silently around the car toward the rocky outcrops. As I came around the back of the car, I saw only a few meters away the horse-like head, long neck, and shoulders of a huge perentie! Immediately, this enormous lizard dove, disappearing instantly down a hole underneath the small tor. This was the first live perentie I had seen. Naturally, I had to make an effort to capture this magnificent beast. I spent the better part of a week doing just that, but came up empty-handed.

Tracks of this big lizard were all around the outcrop as well as around several more deep burrows. The first thing I tried to do was to smoke the lizard out. I shoved a long length of dynamite fuse as far as it would go down into the hole, and lit the end: whoosh! With the fuse sputtering and smoking, great wisps of acrid sulfurous smoke poured out. But no lizard. Next, I decided to try to capture the perentie using nylon snares. Dozens of nooses soon festooned all the major entrances and exits from underneath the rock. We then moved a half kilometer away so as not to disturb the lizard. After a day had passed, I quietly crept up to the tor to check, and found my nooses undisturbed, exactly as I had left them. The lizard had not moved! I left quietly and returned the next day . . . same thing. On the third day, I found one of my nylon nooses frayed and broken. The perentie had been snared but had rubbed the nylon line against the rough granite until it broke! Since it did not look like I would be able to capture the lizard alive, I decided to try to shoot it. Very early the next morning I loaded my .410 shotgun and crept up to the tor . . . Quietly, I positioned myself a few meters above the main entrance and waited silently. For several hours nothing moved except arthropods and an occasional small lizard. There wasn't a sound, except for the ever-present bush flies. Finally it grew hot. About noon, my legs were going to sleep, and I was thirsty, stiff, and cramped so I slowly and quietly got up and moved toward the hole. As I did so, I heard a loud noise and looked up in front of me to see the perentie charging right at me, diving for its hole.[1] The animal went right between my legs in an instant, before I could respond. It looked to be a full two meters long! It must have emerged from another entrance. The next morning I tried again, creeping slowly behind bushes up toward the perentie's lair. From a few hundred meters away, I scanned the outcrop with binoculars and saw the magnificent beast, head held high surveying its kingdom. But as I tried to sneak closer, it vanished down a hole. I never saw that perentie again. Trying to catch a perentie is a humbling experience.

In the spring of 1968, Helen and I returned stateside to Princeton, where I began analyzing data and writing scientific papers about Australian desert lizards. In August 1968, I took a position as assistant professor at the University of Texas in Austin (I now hold an endowed professorship there). We settled down, bought a house, and made our family, producing our full quota of two, both daughters. During 1969–1970, I extended my intercontinental comparisons to include the Kalahari semidesert of southern Africa (see Chapter 10).

A decade later, in June of 1978, I returned to Australia as a Guggenheim Fellow to resume studies, alone at first, then with a couple of assistants. My goal on this second trip was to study just two sites but this time in as great detail as possible so as to better characterize uncommon species. I chose to continue to study one of my earlier sites, the L-area, about 40 km east of Laverton. This site was accessible and was the type locality of half a dozen new species Helen and I had discovered in 1966–1967 (see below). In 1978 I first established Red Sands as a study area. Working hard for half a year from June through early December, my assistants and I had collected about forty species of lizards at Red Sands.

Just before Christmas, Helen and our daughters Karen, then ten, and Gretchen, eight, arrived from Texas. On Christmas Eve, we decorated a little desert *Acacia* shrub alongside our camp at the Laverton study area. Needless to say, to their great delight, Santa Claus found the girls halfway around the world! Celebrating winter holidays down under in the intense heat of midsummer never seems quite right, and one has great difficulty getting into the Christmas spirit (bah, humbug!).

Karen and Gretchen did not want to leave their friends in Austin for a protracted period of time, but were finally convinced to stay down under from mid-December through mid-April. In order to be gone from school for four months, they had to get special permission from their teachers, and they were given reading and work assignments to fill their days abroad. The girls are smart and found that they could do their homework in a few hours each day, leaving them with ample time for fun extracurricular activities. They kept *Moloch* as pets and watched them eat ants. They helped us out geckoing at night. Each morning they played with last night's geckos. The girls climbed trees and built "factories" with fallen marble gum limbs—one of these sported an unusual limb with a couple of right angles that allowed it to be rotated somewhat like a huge rotisserie (they called this "the factory"). A swing provided them with hours of sanctity from the ever-present bush flies. Karen and Gretchen get along famously, and one another's company in the wilderness proved to be more than an adequate social environment. By the time April arrived, the same two girls who a few months before "didn't want to go to Australia for such a long time" had made a complete about-face, and now they "didn't want to go back to Texas."

For my fortieth birthday down under, my clever daughter Karen wrote me the following poem, ably and amply illustrated around the margins with bats, cats, lizards, monkeys, and hats:

> *Pianka, the Pickler,*
> *Is not in right now,*
> *He's out in the barn;*
> *He's picklin' a cow.*
>
> *Pianka, the Pickler,*
> *Has pickled a cat,*
> *He's pickled a bat;*
> *He's pickled his hat!*

Pianka, the Pickler

— Karen Pianka
a birthday
present
for Daddy
Jan. 24, 1979

Pianka, the Pickler
Is not in right now,
He's out in the barn;
He's picklin' a cow.

Pianka, the Pickler
Has pickled a cat,
He's pickled a bat;
He's pickled his hat!

Pianka, the Pickler,
He pickles lizards,
He pickles monkeys
And chicken's gizzards.

Pianka, the Pickler,
The picklin' elf,
If he doesn't watch
out;
He'll pickle himself!

Pianka, the Pickler,
He pickles lizards,
He pickles monkeys
And chicken's gizzards.

Pianka, the Pickler,
The picklin' elf,
If he doesn't watch out;
He'll pickle himself!

Early in 1979, one day at Red Sands I came upon the track of a large perentie. I was extremely surprised, for I had always been under the impression that these animals never strayed too far from rock outcrops. Since this was a study area, and far from rocks, I had to catch this perentie. It turned out to require over two weeks. Following the tracks that first day, I quickly found where the lizard had first spotted me and broken into a run headed directly to a large burrow in the bank of a sandridge. I tried snares to no avail and then sat all day long for several days with the .410, waiting in ambush, but the lizard never left the burrow.

This perentie burrow was located about two kilometers away from camp, out of sight, and over a couple of sandridges. One day, while I was sitting quietly, patiently trying to ambush the perentie with a shotgun, I heard singing in the distance and looked out over the sandplain to see my two daughters coming my way. They had fixed snacks for themselves, and for me, and had decided to go find Daddy. The girls were singing "99 bottles of beer on the wall . . . ," bravely keeping their spirits up as they wandered through the vast desert wilderness. Meanwhile, Helen had been out lizarding on her own—when she returned to camp, and found Karen and Gretchen missing, she was worried sick, for she had left them with strict instructions never ever to get out of earshot of the caravan unless accompanied by adults. She knew I was on an all-day-long stakeout. When the girls and I returned, Helen was furious with them for having the confidence that they could find Daddy out there—they could very easily have misjudged the direction they were going and wandered off into no-man's-land! As long as they stayed on sand, we could always track them down, but if they had wandered far enough, they would have come to hard mulga country, where even expert trackers such as Helen and myself might not have been able to follow their spoor.

Eventually, after several more days of vainly waiting in ambush, I decided that I had no choice but to dig the perentie out. Helen, Karen, Gretchen, and I drove over early one day in Old Lady with supplies of food and water. Using my mirror, I noted that the tunnel went down into the sandridge over a meter and then turned sharply to the right. After measuring the distance to the turn with a stick, I dug a pit at the appropriate place about a meter deep, and found that the burrow turned sharply to the right. After measuring the distance to the next turn with a stick, I dug another pit at the appropriate place about a meter deep down to the burrow again. Then, using another mirror, one of my daughters reflected some sunlight down into the bottom of the pit, where I used my own mirror to peer into the tunnel beyond the first turn. It plowed ahead another couple meters before turning again. So I dug still another pit, deeper this time, down to the burrow, where we repeated the mirror processes a couple more times. Finally, hours later, I was surprised to find that the tunnel turned abruptly upward heading directly toward the other side of a large clump of shrubs. The side of the sandridge was by now covered with large piles of red sand next to several meter-deep holes (the "fossil"

remains of these "digs" are still evident over a dozen years later!). Climbing out of my pit, I went around to the place the tunnel seemed to be heading and found tracks indicating that the perentie had recently exited via a back door! The entire morning would have been a complete waste except for the fact that a rare nocturnal skink crawled out of the perentie burrow into the bottom of one of my pits. Also, my daughters greatly enjoyed the coolness of the digs (the deep holes that I had dug). It underscores what a good deal the lizards have—when it gets too hot, they simply retreat to the cool underground and shut down their thermostats, conserving energy. Homeothermic endotherms, such as birds and large mammals, require much more energy and suffer through the heat of midday. This failure reinforced another lesson learned earlier: never seriously attack the end of a lizard trail unless you are certain that it is in fact the end!

I followed that perentie's tracks again another kilometer or so along the same sandridge to another burrow system, this time a rabbit warren. Again, I set snares, but this time wire ones. Caught a rabbit, but no perentie. I felt like a real hunter-provider, bringing meat home to my family. We ate that rabbit (Karen and Gretchen kept its soft fuzzy pelt, which they enjoyed petting). The next time the perentie moved, it took off cross-country, going about three kilometers directly to yet another large burrow under a small bush. After I had convinced myself that it definitely had not left this third burrow, I set another batch of snares. For a full week I checked the nooses daily, but the big lizard did not move. At last, I decided that once again the time had come to try to exhume the animal. Another daylong festival with the family, shining mirrors, poking sticks, and carefully excavating. After a series of pits, I had followed the tunnel for almost ten meters, when I asked one of my daughters to shine some sunlight down to the bottom of my newest pit (a meter deep). With great joy, only a meter away, I actually saw the perentie's yellow-tipped black tail, spotted with yellow! I exclaimed, "We have it now," and carefully resumed digging. When I reached its hind legs, I hog-tied them together (I wasn't about to take any chances that this lizard might get away at this point). I put on a long-sleeved shirt and leather gloves in case the perentie got aggressive and fought back. At last I held the great beast aloft for all to see (Helen captured this moment of triumph on film). As we began to make our way back to our campsite with the perentie, Karen broke out into spontaneous song, joyously singing:

Oh, re-joice, the pe- ren- tie is got! Oh, re-joice, the pe- ren- tie is got! The migh-ty

liz-ard, as great as a bliz-zard Oh, re- joice, the pe- ren- tie is got!

Oh, rejoice, the perentie is got!
Oh, rejoice, the perentie is got!
The mighty lizard, as great as a blizzard . . .
Oh, rejoice, the perentie is got! {repeat}

She had been mentally composing this perentie song all the while I dug. She commented later with some dismay that only three words, gizzard, blizzard, and wizard, rhymed with lizard! We christened that day, February 3, "perentie day" forever after.

I chilled the great beast down overnight in a wet cloth bag, and the next day, after weighing and measuring him (he had everted his hemipenes for us, allowing me to determine his sex), Karen and Gretchen each drew his portrait. Then we photographed him and finally released him. But he would not make a break for it, and just lay as if dead under the shrub where I put him even after he had warmed up. Eventually, we left him there playing possum. Returning a few hours later, I found he had gone—tracks headed right back toward where we had exhumed him. I got my camera and followed the track to take pictures of the trail he left. Just to see if I could do it, I tracked him down a second time, this time catching him above ground away from burrows. He had walked and run about two kilometers from the point of release. Following an abortive escape attempt to outrun me, he went into a state known to physiologists as "oxygen debt" and held his ground at bay, this time inflating his throat and hissing, flickering his great long tongue at me. After a few more final pictures, I said "Good-bye, old buddy," and finally left the great lizard to his own devices once and for all. With his tail, this lizard was as long as Helen is tall: 5 feet 4 1/2 inches.

About a month later, the four of us and a new field assistant named François spent the heat of a stifling hot midday at a muddy billabong (a stagnant pool) called Reetz Creek, getting wet and cooling off.

Lizarding

Karen and Gretchen were still in their underwear playing in the murky water, while Helen, François, and I were relaxing after a dunk, sitting on the bank enjoying a cool beer. In my peripheral vision, I saw movement behind me and turned to look. At first glance I thought it was a cat, but immediately recognized a medium-sized perentie only a few meters behind us. As soon as I moved, the lizard instantly took off running, and the three of us jumped up and took chase. It easily lost us, but I started tracking it to see where the perentie had disappeared to and determined that it must have taken refuge in a second, much smaller and shallower, billabong alongside the deeper one we were enjoying. (This perentie was probably coming in for a drink when it came upon us sitting quietly.) François claimed that he could capture the perentie in the water, explaining that he had caught *Varanus* in his native South Africa that way. Soon he was down on his hands and knees moving slowly around the small billabong, feeling around in the muddy water for the lizard. François proclaimed, "I feel it!" and the next thing we knew he held up a medium-sized perentie. As François climbed out of the water holding the lizard, I broke out singing Karen's perentie song and was quickly accompanied by Helen, Karen, and Gretchen (François was greatly impressed, for he knew nothing of the pageantry that accompanies the rare event of capturing a perentie!).

This was a small to medium-sized perentie, only about a meter and a half in total length. We took pictures of each of us holding the perentie by its neck and pelvic region, and then decided to try to get some photographs of the lizard on the ground. As soon as I put it down, it became extremely aggressive and began lunging at me with mouth agape, hissing and threatening (I held its tail and simply put my foot on the lizard to subdue it). That was when François had his great idea to be photographed with the lizard hanging on, dangling by its mouth from his hand. "You've got to be kidding," I said. "No," François insisted adamantly, explaining that he had done this with South African *Varanus*, and he wanted to have a matching picture with a big Australian *Varanus*. I told him perenties have very sharp teeth that can injure a fragile hand. But François said not to worry, he knew where the animal could bite without doing any serious damage to the soft, fleshy palm. Neither of us thought about the unprotected back side of his hand. (The savanna monitor of southern Africa is not a meat eater and has very different peglike crushing teeth.) After a little further argument, I agreed to take François's picture with his camera while he posed with the lizard biting his hand. He set his camera, showed me which button to push, and handed me his camera. Then I took my foot off the lizard, continuing to hold on to its tail, and it began again to lunge ferociously at us, open-mouthed. François bravely got down on one knee and carefully placed the fleshy palm and tender back side of his hand directly into the perentie's mouth. The lizard immediately clamped down hard, crunching first on one side of its mouth, and then on the other. François blanched white, fell limp with great pain, and began cursing in his native Afrikaans. The perentie had a bulldog's grip on his hand. I didn't know quite what to do to get the lizard off, but suggested that if we put the perentie into the water, it might let go of its own volition, minimizing further damage. This we did, and when the perentie realized that it was free to depart, it did indeed release its hold on François's savaged hand and swam away into the murky depths like a crocodile. It was strange to see a desert lizard so at home in the water! (Unfortunately, in the panic of the moment, we neglected to take any pictures!)

Perenties eat carrion, such as road-killed kangaroos, and their mouths harbor a wide variety of noxious bacteria, effectively making them almost venomous. Their teeth are long and very sharp, with serrated cutting edges (the teeth don't look that impressive when a perentie gapes at you because they are largely hidden in soft gum tissue, but they are nearly 10 mm long). François's bite quickly became badly infected so that we soon began to fear blood poisoning. We drove him into Laverton, where he caught the next Royal Flying Doctor flight to the hospital in Kalgoorlie. A week later we picked him up with his arm in a sling, the infection cured. The perentie's sharp teeth had severed some of the tendons to François's fingers on the back side of his hand. François was a musician, and to regain the use of his partially paralyzed hand, he later had to undergo restorative surgery to get his tendons reconnected. This was not the most foolish thing one of my field assistants ever did—a young know-it-all in North America once picked up a large, and very dangerous, Mojave green rattlesnake with his bare hands, thinking that it was a harmless bull snake. Luckily, he had grasped the sleeping snake right behind the head and held on tight when it rattled! He would have been killed if that rattlesnake had struck his hand as he reached for it from directly in front of the coiled snake. On another occasion, an assistant wandered off and got lost in the Great Victoria Desert, but fortunately found a track and, with really incredible luck, managed to hitch a ride back to camp just as I was becoming extremely concerned. I have never lost a field assistant . . . yet!

I myself was bitten by a medium-sized perentie in early February of 1991 while helping a new assistant photograph the lizard. He wanted to get a picture of the perentie on the ground as I stood by, watching. The lizard dashed behind me and began to climb up the back of my leg. I had visions of it climbing up to my head and scratching my face with its large, sharp claws. My naïve assistant, who could see the lizard and could have grabbed it, stood by fearfully, awestruck, doing nothing (he could have gone around behind me and grabbed the lizard). Reflexively, I reached my left arm around behind my back to try to get the lizard off. It chomped down on my left wrist with its six-to-eight-millimeter serrated cutting teeth. My assistant remained frozen in awe as I began bleeding profusely. Then I reached around with my right arm in a continuing effort to try to extricate the lizard, whereupon it clamped down on my right thumb and began to chew. It hurt! By the time my assistant finally came to my rescue, I was slashed up and bleeding like a stuck pig. Fortunately for me, no tendons were severed.

I washed the bites in alcohol and bandaged them to keep the flies out. They healed over, and I thought I had recovered. But a few days later, I got bitten again on the same poor thumb by a much smaller *Varanus tristis* (teeth about 3–4 mm), which also chewed. My thumb got infected, and then the left wrist went sympathetic and got infected, too. Luckily, we had some antibiotics, and after taking them for a couple of days, the swelling went down and I thought I was going to be OK (Aussies and Aborigines say that a goanna bite never heals). But my thumb swelled up again a month later to twice its normal size. Apparently, blood-born antibiotics do not easily reach poorly vascularized synovial joint capsules. Five prescriptions of different antibiotics later, the infection was still not completely cured. There are two morals to this story: (1) don't stand still around a monitor lizard, and (2) if you should ever be so unfortunate as to find a monitor lizard on your back side, whatever you do, don't put your arms around behind your back to try to get it off. Instead, lie down on your belly, and let it walk or run away by itself. Isn't twenty-twenty hindsight great?

On my fourth trip down under, I was driving along in Katy, another Toyota Land Cruiser, towing all my creature comforts behind me—a propane fridge and stove in a small house trailer (termed a "caravan" or "van" down under). Suddenly, from the edge of the track, a huge perentie came running at full tilt, careening right down the center of the track, head held high, on a collision course with Katy's front end. (Unlike other lizards that have the primitive tetrapod arrangement of their limbs held out to their sides, large *Varanus* hold their legs underneath themselves and walk erect like a mammal. Perenties have exceedingly long necks and can hold their heads up quite high.) I was going much too fast to stop, but I braked hard, fully expecting to hit the lizard. But, at the very last moment, the perentie ducked underneath the car and van.

On my penultimate trip down under in late 1990, I came upon the second largest perentie I have yet encountered, a full 1.8 meters in total length. This was an almost mystical experience with a perentie, as its track suddenly became the magnificent animal, frozen in mid-stride. How I wished that I had my camera at that moment!

Phylogenetic relationships of Australian lizards are of considerable interest, but largely unknown. Systematics and modern molecular biology have produced techniques, such as DNA sequencing, that allow the reconstruction of phylogenies ("family trees") from tissue samples of all taxa concerned. On a recent expedition, I froze individually labeled hearts and livers from a large series of many hundreds of lizards, representing dozens of different species, in a canister of liquid nitrogen. We will use these tissues to isolate and amplify DNA, which will be sequenced to acquire data that can be used to recover probable phylogenies.

In 1966, the taxonomy of Australian desert lizards was in shambles. There were only three books on the subject—Glauert's *Handbook of the Lizards of Western Australia*, Waite's *Reptiles and Amphibians of South Australia*, and Worrell's *Reptiles of Australia*—and none was adequate. Right from the beginning, I encountered lizards for which I couldn't find names, especially *Ctenotus* skinks. As time went on, I developed my own set of operative code names for these species, designed to be clear and distinctive. A pretty little blue-tailed skink became "cyanurus," a very similar species but without the blue tail was "acyanurus," a copper-tailed sandridge species was "cupreicaudus," another small red sandridge species was "arenicola" (sand loving), a small *Ctenotus* species was "minutus" (tiny), a large species of *Ctenotus* was "giganteus," and so on.

It soon became apparent that about half a dozen species had never been properly described by scientists and needed official new scientific names. This was surprising as well as exciting, since at the time, most biologists were of the opinion that almost all species of vertebrates had already been named (we know now that many species of Amazonian vertebrates still remain to be described and named). I briefly considered naming some of these new species myself, but thought better of it since I am not a trained taxonomist or systematist (mistakes can foul up taxonomy for years to come). So, one day in 1967, I took a dozen jars containing hundreds of *Ctenotus*, sorted by my own unofficial code names, to a real systematist, the late Dr. Glen Storr, then curator of herpetology at the Western Australian Museum.

Storr went through all my material plus all that on hand in the museum, carefully studying the specimens and counting their scales. He concurred with me that my "species" were good species, and that some of my new species were undescribed, but he did manage to find proper names for several. My "acyanurus" was *Ctenotus colletti*, "arenicola" was *Ctenotus brooksi*, "cupreicaudus" was *Ctenotus leae*, and "minutus" was *Ctenotus schomburgkii*. Several other species that I had been using given names for were not the species I thought but were, in fact, unrecognized new species. He found seven previously undescribed species in my collection. To my intense disappointment, he chose not to use any of my code names; my "giganteus" became *grandis*, whereas my "cyanurus" (blue tail) became *calurus* (pretty tail). Storr named three others *ariadnae*, *atlas*, and *dux*, the first after a museum librarian who had helped him to get obscure references, and the other two as Latin words that hint at two type localities, Atley Homestead and Dunges Table Hill.

One day, before he had chosen any of these new names, Glen took me aside when Helen wasn't around and asked me which of the seven undescribed species she had specialized on (i.e., which one did she seem to catch much more often than I did?). I promptly identified a very wary, large, and handsome greenish skink, which favors messy spinifex and litter areas under marble gums. Helen developed a real knack in staking out and patiently waiting, gun cocked, for these cryptic big green trophies to show themselves (we had erroneously been calling these *Ctenotus leusueri*, a name belonging to a relative). Appropriately, Storr bestowed on this magnificent new lizard species the name *Ctenotus helenae* in Helen's honor.

Unbeknownst to me, he had taken her aside, too, but this time had asked "which one did Eric specialize on?" She identified a small but wary spinifex skink, one that we had found to be extremely difficult to collect. After learning that these skinks are active during the heat of midday, I spent many a determined hour out in the hot sun leaning against my shovel as the third leg of a tripod, on alert, with my gun cocked, bush flies swarming around my face, poised and waiting for movement in a spinifex tussock to which a small skink had run. Although I managed to collect a mere eleven specimens, that was as many as there were in all the major Australian museums at that time. Because these lizards appeared to key out to *Ctenotus colletti*, that was what I was calling them, but in fact it was an undescribed species. Storr designated this cryptic little skink *Ctenotus piankai*, my official namesake. It is a great honor to have a species named after me, particularly a lizard! People will have to use my name long after I am dead and forgotten! Since then, I have discovered that *Ctenotus piankai* are really fairly abundant and can be trapped in pit traps using drift fences. During the past few years, I have managed to collect hundreds of these elusive little lizards. I look forward to writing a scientific paper on the biology of this species soon!

Note to Chapter 3

1. Sometimes when a large *Varanus* is surprised in open country, it runs right toward a person and climbs up, apparently thinking that he or she is a tree. This can be rather startling, and the victim can get quite scratched up! (This happened to me once with a medium-sized perentie, and I received some painful bites trying to get it off my back.)

LIZARD NATURAL HISTORY

Four

How organisms go about their daily activities and how they use their environments are of great interest to ecologists. The various ways in which organisms conform to the conditions imposed upon them by their surroundings are known as adaptations. All aspects of an animal's behavior are important—natural history includes spatial and temporal patterns of activity, thermoregulation, foraging behavior, diet, courtship, mating, and reproduction, as well as escape from predators.

USE OF TIME AND SPACE: THERMAL RELATIONS

Animals that maintain relatively constant internal body temperatures are known as homeotherms, whereas those whose temperature varies widely from time to time, often approximating the temperature of their immediate environment, are called poikilotherms. A related pair of useful terms are sometimes confused with these two terms. An ectotherm obtains its heat from its external environment, whereas an endotherm produces most of its own heat internally by means of oxidative metabolism. All plants, and the vast majority of animals, are ectothermic; the only continuously endothermic animals are birds and mammals (some of these become ectothermic at times). Certain poikilotherms, including large snakes and large lizards, are at times at least partially endothermic, too. Many ectothermic lizards actually regulate their body temperatures very precisely during periods of activity by appropriate behavioral means, thus achieving a degree of homeothermy. An active desert lizard may have a body temperature every bit as high as that of a bird or mammal (the layperson's misleading terms "warm-blooded" and "cold-blooded" should be abandoned).

Lizards constitute an extremely conspicuous element of the vertebrate faunas of most deserts, especially warmer ones. Indeed, the Australian mammalogist H. H. Finlayson (1943) referred to the vast interior deserts of Australia as "a land of lizards." Ectothermy facilitates metabolic inactivity, allowing lizards to capitalize on scant, unpredictable food supplies. Moreover, along with other ectotherms, lizards are low-energy animals. One day's food supply for a small bird will last a lizard of the same weight for a month or more. Ectothermy thus has distinct advantages over endothermy under the harsh and unpredictable conditions that prevail in deserts. By means of this thermal tactic, lizards can conserve water and energy by becoming inactive during the heat of midday, during resource shortages, or whenever difficult physical conditions occur (such as during heat waves or droughts). Birds and mammals must weather these inhospitable periods at a substantially higher metabolic cost. Hence ectothermy confers a competitive advantage on lizards over endotherms in desert environments.

In temperate zones, hot arid regions typically support rich lizard faunas, whereas cooler forested areas have many fewer lizard species and individuals. Lizards can enjoy the benefits of a high metabolic rate during relatively brief periods when conditions are appropriate for activity, yet still become inactive during adverse conditions. By facilitating metabolic inactivity on both a daily and a seasonal basis, poikilothermy allows lizards to capitalize on unpredictable food supplies. Moreover, lizards can effectively reduce temporal heterogeneity by retreating underground, becoming inactive, and lowering their metabolic rate during harsh periods (some desert rodents estivate when food or water is in short supply). Poikilothermy may well contribute to the apparent relative success of lizards over birds and mammals in arid regions. Temperate zone forests and grasslands are probably too shady and too cold for ectothermic lizards to be very successful because these animals depend on basking to reach body temperatures high enough for activity; birds and mammals, in contrast, do quite well in such areas partly because of their endothermy. Lizards do well in warm tropical forests, however.

A spectacular example of the capacity of lizards to go dormant took place in Arizona during the 1960s. An instant "Sun City" was built in the Sonoran desert. This small town had been in place for several years without appreciable rainfall, but the local residents had planted lawns and trees, which were irrigated with ground water pumped up from the water table. When massive August rains finally fell, Gila monsters began popping up out of the ground in people's yards— these lizards had been buried underground, inactive, living off the stored fat in their tails during the time that the city was being built.

When averaged over a long enough period of time, the heat gained by an animal must be exactly balanced by the heat lost back to its environment; otherwise the animal would either warm up or cool off. Many different pathways of heat gains and heat losses exist. Balancing a heat budget requires very different adaptations under varying environmental conditions. At different times of day, ambient thermal conditions may change from being too cold to being too warm for a particular animal's optimal performance. Animals living in hot deserts must avoid overheating by being able to minimize heat loads and to dissipate heat efficiently; in contrast, those that live in colder places, such as at high altitudes and high latitudes, must be adept at acquiring and retaining heat.

Environmental temperatures fluctuate in characteristic ways at different places over the earth's surface, both daily and seasonally. In the absence of a long-term warming or cooling trend, environmental temperatures at any given place remain roughly constant when averaged over an entire annual cycle. The range in temperature within a year is much greater at high latitudes than it is nearer the equator. An animal could balance its annual heat budget by being entirely passive and simply allowing its temperature to mirror that of its environment. Such a passive thermoregulator is known as a thermoconformer. Of course, it is also an ectotherm. Another extreme tactic is to maintain an absolutely constant body temperature by physiological, and/or behavioral means, dissipating (or avoiding) excess bodily heat during warm periods but retaining (or gaining) heat during cooler periods. Such organisms that carefully regulate their internal temperatures are thermoregulators. Both endotherms and ectotherms regulate their body temperatures. There is a continuum between the two extremes of perfect conformity and perfect regulation. Regulation is never perfect. Because thermoregulation clearly has costs and risks as well as profits, there is an optimal level of regulation that depends on the precise form of the constraints, and on the interactions between costs and benefits arising from a particular ecological situation.

Thermoregulation often involves both physiological and behavioral adjustments; as an example of the latter, consider a typical terrestrial diurnal desert lizard. During the early morning, when ambient temperatures are low, such a lizard locates itself in warmer microclimates of the environmental thermal mosaic (for example, in a small depression in the open or on a sunny tree trunk), basking in the sun with its body as perpendicular as possible to the sun's rays, thereby maximizing heat gained. With the daily march of temperature, ambient temperatures quickly rise, and the lizard seeks cooler shady microhabitats. Individuals of some species retreat into burrows as temperatures rise; others climb up off the ground into cooler air and orient themselves facing into the sun's rays, thereby reducing heat load. Many lizards change colors, and thus their heat-reflective properties; they turn dark and heat absorbent at colder times of day but pale and heat reflective at hotter times. Such adjustments allow individual lizards to be active over a longer period of time than they could be if they conformed passively to ambient thermal conditions; presumably, these lizards are also more effective competitors and better able to elude predators as a result of such thermoregulatory behaviors.

Thermoregulation in lizards is not as simple as it might first seem, for it encompasses a wide diversity of very different thermoregulatory tactics among species, ranging from ectothermic poikilothermy to, and including, ectothermic homeothermy. Even a casual observer quickly notices that various species of desert lizards differ markedly in their times and places of activity. Some species are active early in the morning, but others do not emerge until late morning or midday. Most geckos and pygopodids, and some Australian skinks, are nocturnal. Certain species are climbers, others subterranean, while still others are strictly surface dwellers. Among the latter, some tend to be found in open areas, whereas others frequent the edges of vegetation. Thermal relations of active lizards vary widely among species and are profoundly influenced by their spatial and temporal patterns of activity. Body temperatures of some diurnal species average 38°C or higher, whereas those of nocturnal species are typically in the mid-twenties, closely paralleling ambient air temperatures.

Interesting differences between species also occur in the variance in body temperature as well as in the relationship between body temperatures and air temperatures. For example, among North American lizards, two arboreal species (*Urosaurus graciosus* and *Sceloporus magister*) display narrower variances in body temperature than do terrestrial species on the same study sites. Presumably, arboreal habits often facilitate efficient, economic, and rather precise thermoregulation. Climbing lizards have only to shift position slightly to be in the sun or shade, or on a warmer or cooler substrate, and normally do not move through a diverse thermal environment. Moreover, arboreal lizards need not expend energy making long runs as do most ground-dwellers, and thus climbing species do not raise their body temperatures metabolically to as great an extent as do terrestrial lizards.

Such differences in temporal patterns of activity, the use of space, and body temperature relationships are hardly independent. Rather, they complexly constrain one another, sometimes in intricate and obscure ways. For example, thermal conditions associated with particular microhabitats change in characteristic ways in time: a choice basking site at one time of day becomes an inhospitable hot spot at another time. Perches of arboreal lizards receive full sun early and late in the day when ambient air temperatures tend to be low, and basking is therefore desirable, but these same tree trunks are shady and cool during the heat of midday when heat avoidance behavior becomes necessary. In contrast, the fraction of the ground's surface in the sun is low early and late when shadows are long, but reaches a maximum at midday. Terrestrial heliothermic lizards may thus experience a shortage of suitable basking sites early and late in the day; moreover, during the heat of the day, their movements through relatively extensive patches of open sun can be severely curtailed. Hence ground-dwelling lizards encounter fundamentally different, and more difficult, thermal challenges than do climbing species.

Radiation, convection, and conduction are the most important means of heat exchange for the majority of diurnal lizards, although the thermal background in which these processes occur is strongly influenced by prevailing air temperatures. Ambient air temperatures are critical to nocturnal lizards as well as to certain very cryptic diurnal species. In an analysis of the costs and benefits of lizard thermoregulatory strategies, Huey and Slatkin (1976) identified the slope of the regression of body temperature against ambient environmental temperature as a useful indicator (in this case, an inverse

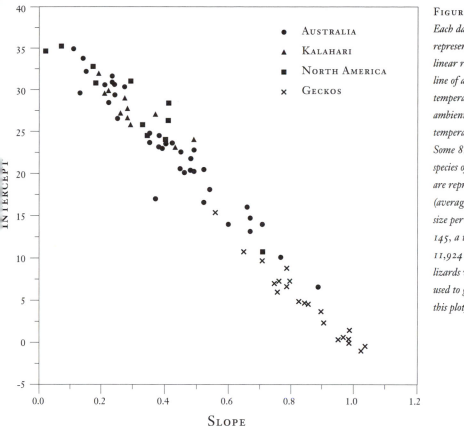

FIGURE 5

Each data point represents the linear regression line of active body temperature on ambient air temperature. Some 82 different species of lizard are represented (average sample size per species is 145, a total of 11,924 individual lizards were used to generate this plot).

measure) of the degree of passivity in regulation of body temperature. On such a plot of active body temperature versus ambient temperature, a slope of one indicates true poikilothermy or totally passive thermoconformity (a perfect correlation between air temperature and body temperature results), whereas a slope of zero reflects the other extreme of perfect thermoregulation. Lizards span this entire thermoregulation spectrum: among active diurnal heliothermic species, regressions of body temperature on air temperature are fairly flat (for several species, including some quite small ones, slopes do not differ significantly from zero); among nocturnal species, slopes of similar plots are typically closer to unity. Various other species (nocturnal, diurnal, and crepuscular), particularly Australian ones, are intermediate, filling in this continuum of thermoregulatory tactics.

A straight line can be represented as a single point in the coordinates of slope versus intercept; these two parameters are plotted for linear regressions of body temperatures on air temperatures among some eighty-two species of lizards in Figure 5. Each data point represents the least-squares linear regression of body temperature against air temperature for a given species of desert lizard. Interestingly enough, these data points fall on another, transcendent, straight line. The position of any particular species along this spectrum reflects a great deal about its complex activities in space and time. The line plotted offers a potent linear dimension on which various species can be placed in attempts to formulate general schemes of lizard ecology. Various other ecological parameters, including reproductive tactics, can be mapped onto this emergent spatial-temporal axis. The intriguing "intercept" of the intercepts (38.8°C) approximates the point of intersection of all eighty-two regression lines and presumably represents an innate design constraint imposed by lizard physiology and metabolism. It is no accident that this value also corresponds more or less to our own body temperatures, and indeed, to those of all mammals!

Most, but not all, lizards have a small, light-sensitive third eye midway between their two lateral eyes located beneath the parietal scale on top of their head. This third eye is thought to serve as a dosimeter of solar radiation, and sensory input from it is integrated with hormones to control the daily cycle of activity, or circadian rhythm (i.e., the lizard's "biological clock"). Not all reptiles possess the parietal eye—it is lacking in turtles, snakes, and crocodilians and is not present in several families of lizards (Teiidae, Gekkonidae, and Helodermatidae). Birds and mammals do not have this third eye either.

FEEDING ECOLOGY

In an environment with a scant food supply, a consumer cannot afford to bypass many inferior prey items because mean search time per item encountered is long, and expectation of prey encounter is low. In such an environment, a broad diet maximizes returns per unit expenditure, favoring generalization. In a food-rich environment, however, search time per item is reduced since a foraging animal encounters numerous potential prey items; under such circumstances, substandard prey

Eric caught his first Varanus gouldi *by chasing it up a tree and then noosing it with a fishing pole while standing on top of Matilda's top carrier (1966)*

Old Lady at a recently burned area east of Neale Junction (1978)

Diplodactylus ciliaris, *an arboreal gecko, sporting a slightly satanic smile*

Diplodactylus
pulcher, *the
beautiful gecko, on
Helen's hand*

Ctenotus
helenae, *Helen's
namesake*

Karen and
Gretchen sketch
the perentie
(1979)

Nephrurus levis,
*a species of knob-
tailed gecko found
on sandplains*

*Baobab bottle tree
in the Kimberley*

*White marble
gums against blue
skies on the L-area*

*Nephrurus
laevissimus,
a sandridge
knob-tailed gecko,
hissing and
lunging in
defensive posture*

Road sign in
Australia

Tiliqua rugosa,
the bobtail, waving
its blue tongue in
typical display

items can be bypassed economically because the expectation of finding a superior item in the near future is high. Hence rich food supplies are expected to favor selective foraging and to lead to narrow diets. In reality, of course, food abundances are ever changing, both spatially and temporally.

Certain species of lizards are dietary specialists, eating only a very narrow range of prey items. For example, the Australian agamid *Moloch horridus* eats essentially nothing except ants, mostly of a single species of *Iridomyrmex* (North American horned lizards, genus *Phrynosoma*, are also ant specialists). Other lizard species are termite specialists, including the Australian nocturnal geckos *Diplodactylus conspicillatus* and *Rhynchoedura ornata*, plus some species of diurnal *Ctenotus* skinks, as well as the Kalahari lacertid *Heliobolus lugubris* and fossorial (subterranean) *Typhlosaurus* skinks. Even though these species eat virtually nothing but isoptera, specialization on termites and ants is economically feasible because these social insects normally occur in a clumped spatial distribution, and hence constitute a concentrated source of food. Still other lizard species, though not quite so specialized, also have narrow diets. For example, the beautiful Kalahari lacertid *Nucras tessellata* and the Australian pygopodid *Pygopus nigriceps* both consume considerably more scorpions than do other lizard species. *Nucras* forages widely to capture these large arachnids by day in their diurnal retreats, whereas the nocturnal *Pygopus* sits and waits for scorpions at night above ground during the latter's normal period of activity.[1] While scorpions are solitary prey items, they are extremely large and nutritious, presumably facilitating evolution of dietary specialization.

For similar reasons, specialization on other lizards as food items has evolved in the North American *Crotaphytus wislizeni* as well as among most Australian *Varanus*. Other species of lizards eat a considerably wider variety of foods. Dietary diversity also varies within species from time to time and from place to place as the composition of diets changes, with opportunistic feeding in response to fluctuating prey abundances and availabilities. However, the consistency of lizard diets over space and time is fairly remarkable, suggesting a profound impact of microhabitat utilization, foraging mode, as well as various anatomical, historical (phylogenetic), and behavioral constraints.

Another, more extreme, example of this phenomenon occurs after heavy summer rains when termites send out their winged reproductives in great abundance, and virtually every species of lizard eats nothing but termites (even lizard species that normally never consume termites). During such fleeting moments of great prey abundance, there is little competition for food, and dietary overlap among members of a desert lizard fauna is sometimes nearly complete.[2]

Biologically significant variation occurs between species in utilization of certain relatively minor food categories: for example, in the diets of climbing lizard species, hemipterans-homopterans and mantids-phasmids as well as various flying insects (wasps, Diptera, and Lepidoptera) tend to be better represented than they are among terrestrial species. Likewise, geckos tend to consume more nocturnal arthropods (scorpions, crickets, roaches, and moths) than do most diurnal species (however, certain diurnal lizards, such as *Nucras* mentioned above, do capture nocturnal prey in their diurnal retreats). Such prey items are thus indicators of spatial and temporal patterns of activity.

Only a relatively few food types dominate diets of desert lizards. Prey resource spectra are broadly similar between the three continents, although notable quantitative differences occur. In North America, the seven most important food types (totaling 84 percent), in decreasing order by volumetric importance, are: beetles, termites, insect larvae, grasshoppers plus crickets, ants, plant materials, and vertebrates. In the Kalahari, just three food categories far outweigh all others (total 71 percent): termites, beetles, and ants. In Australia, the five most important categories (total 77 percent, in decreasing order) are: vertebrates, termites, ants, grasshoppers plus crickets, and beetles. Three categories, termites, beetles, and ants, constitute major prey items in all three continental desert-lizard systems. Termites assume a disproportionate role in the Kalahari, as do vertebrate foods in Australia (largely a reflection of the diets of varanids).

Many predators attack their prey from ambush, but others usually hunt while on the move. These two modes of foraging have been called the "sit-and-wait" versus the "widely foraging" tactic, respectively. Of course, this dichotomy is somewhat artificial, although numerous animal groups seem to fall rather naturally into one category or the other. Members of most lizard families typically exploit one or the other of these two modes of foraging; thus iguanines, agamids, and geckos primarily sit and wait for their prey, whereas teiids and most skinks forage widely. Lacertids, however, use both modes of foraging, even within closely related species.[3] Certain dietary differences are associated with this apparent dichotomy in foraging tactics. Sit-and-wait predators rely largely on moving prey, whereas widely foraging predators encounter and consume nonmoving types of prey items more frequently.

In order for the sit-and-wait tactic to pay off, prey must be relatively mobile, and prey density must be high (or predator energy requirements low). The success of the widely foraging tactic is also influenced by prey mobility and prey density as well as by the predator's energetic requirements (which should usually be higher than those of sit-and-wait predators), but the searching abilities of the predator and the spatial distribution of its prey assume substantial importance. North American and Australian desert study sites support similar numbers of species of sit-and-wait foragers, whereas this mode of foraging is distinctly impoverished in the Kalahari. Markedly fewer species forage widely in western North America (only one species, a teiid) and in the Kalahari (an average of four species per site) than in the Australian deserts (the mean number of widely foraging species per area is ten, most of which are skinks in the genus *Ctenotus*). Intercontinental comparisons of proportions of total species with various foraging modes are also instructive: a full 60 percent of North American lizard species are sit-and-wait foragers, compared with only 16 percent in the Kalahari and 18 percent in Australia. Percentages of widely foraging species are 14 percent (North America), 27 percent (Kalahari), and 36 percent (Australia).

ADAPTIVE SUITES

Now consider one of these dietary specialists in somewhat greater detail. North American desert horned lizards, *Phrynosoma platyrhinos*, are ant specialists, eating little else. Various features of their anatomy, behavior, diet, temporal pattern of activity, thermoregulation, and reproductive tactics can be profitably interrelated and interpreted to provide an integrated view of the ecology of these interesting lizards (Figure 6).

Ants are small, and contain much undigestible chitin, so that large numbers of them must be consumed. Hence an ant specialist must possess a large stomach for its body size. The stomach of this horned lizard averages about 13 percent of the animal's overall body mass, a

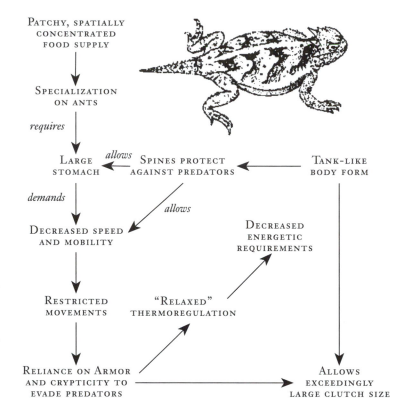

PATCHY, SPATIALLY
CONCENTRATED
FOOD SUPPLY

↓

SPECIALIZATION
ON ANTS

requires

↓

LARGE   *allows*   SPINES PROTECT   ←   TANK-LIKE
STOMACH   AGAINST PREDATORS   BODY FORM

demands   *allows*

↓   DECREASED
                  ENERGETIC
                  REQUIREMENTS

DECREASED SPEED
AND MOBILITY

↓

RESTRICTED   "RELAXED"
MOVEMENTS   THERMOREGULATION

↓

RELIANCE ON ARMOR   ALLOWS
AND CRYPTICITY TO   →   EXCEEDINGLY
EVADE PREDATORS   LARGE CLUTCH SIZE

FIGURE 6
*Diagrammatic
portrayal of factors
influencing the
ecology and body
form of the desert
horned lizard,*
Phrynosoma
platyrhinos

substantially larger fraction than stomachs of other lizard species, even among herbivorous lizards (in six other sympatric North American lizard species, stomach volumes average only 6.4 percent of body weight; among eight Australian species selected as crude ecological counterparts, the ratio of stomach volume to body weight averages only 5.9 percent). *Phrynosoma*'s large stomach requires a tank-like body form, reducing speed and decreasing the lizard's ability to escape from predators by movement. As a result, natural selection has favored a spiny body form and cryptic behavior rather than a sleek body and rapid movement to cover, as in the majority of other lizards. Long periods of exposure while foraging in the open presumably increase risks of predation. A reluctance to move, even when actually threatened by a potential predator, is advantageous under such circumstances. Movement might attract the predator's attention and negate the advantage of concealing coloration and contour. Such decreased movement contributes to the observed high variability in body temperature of *Phrynosoma platyrhinos*, which is significantly greater than that of all other sympatric species of lizards.

Wide fluctuations in horned lizard body temperatures under natural conditions presumably reflect both their long activity period, and perhaps their reduced movements into or out of the sun and shade (most active *Phrynosoma* are in the open sun when first encountered). A consequence is that more time is made available for activities such as eating (foraging ant eaters must spend considerable time feeding). To make use of this patchy and spatially concentrated, but at the same time not overly nutritious, food supply, *Phrynosoma platyrhinos* has evolved a unique constellation of adaptations (an "adaptive suite") that includes its large stomach, spiny tank-like body form, expanded period of activity, and "relaxed" thermoregulation. Another spin-off of the *Phrynosoma* adaptive suite concerns their extraordinarily high investment in reproduction. Females of some species of horned lizards devote as much as 35 percent of their body weight to production of a very large clutch of eggs. This is presumably a simple and direct consequence of their robust body form: lizards that must be able to move rapidly to escape from predators would hardly be expected to weight themselves down with eggs to the same extent as animals like horned lizards that rely almost entirely upon spines and camouflage to avoid their enemies.

REPRODUCTIVE TACTICS

Most lizards lay eggs, but some species retain their eggs internally and give birth to living young. Live-bearing has arisen repeatedly among squamates (lizards and their close relatives, snakes), even multiple times within a single genus. Live-bearing and egg retention are especially prevalent in cooler regions at high elevations and high latitudes. Average clutch size varies from one to nearly fifty among different species of lizards. Some species reproduce only once every second or third year, others but once each year, and still others lay two or more clutches each year.

Lizards that lay only one egg or give birth to a single young include the American polychrid genus *Anolis*, the Kalahari skink *Typhlosaurus gariepensis*, and the geckos *Gehyra variegata*, *G. purpurascens*, and *Ptenopus garrulus*. Clutch size is fixed at one or two eggs in certain families (Geckos, Pygopodids) and genera (*Anolis*). Across all species, the modal clutch size among lizards is two eggs. In the Kalahari agamid *Agama hispida*, clutch size averages 13. Clutch sizes in certain horned lizards are still larger, averaging 24.3 in the American phrynosomatid *Phrynosoma cornutum* (the Texas horned lizard). One of the most fecund lizards is the iguanian *Ctenosaura pectinata*, one female of which had 49 eggs in her oviducts.

Substantial spatial and temporal variation in clutch size also exists within species. In the double-clutched Australian agamid species *Ctenophorus isolepis*, the size of 67 first clutches (August–December) averaged 3.0 eggs, whereas the mean of 41 second clutches (January–February) was 3.9. Females increase in size during the season, and as in many lizards, larger females tend to lay larger clutches. Females also appear to invest relatively more on their second clutches than they do on their first clutch: among 25 first clutches, clutch volumes average only 11 percent of female weight, but in 15 second clutches, the average is 15 percent.

Changes in fecundity with fluctuations in food supplies and local conditions from year to year or location to location have also frequently been observed. In many species, females tend to lay larger clutches in years with above-average precipitation, and presumably ample food supplies.

Clutch or litter mass (either weight or volume), expressed as a fraction of a female's total body weight, also known as "relative clutch mass," ranges from as little as 4–5 percent in some species to as much as 20–30 percent in others. Clutch weights tend to be particularly high in some of the North American horned lizards (genus *Phrynosoma*). Ratios of clutch/litter weight to female body weight correlate strongly with various energetic measures, and can be used as crude indices of a female's instantaneous investment in current reproduction.

In addition to clutch size and female total investment in reproduction, the size (or weight) of an individual oviductal egg or newborn progeny also varies widely among lizards from as little as 1–2 percent in some species to a full 17 percent in the live-bearing Kalahari fossorial skink *Typhlosaurus gariepensis*. Such expenditures per progeny are inverse measures of the extent to which a juvenile lizard must grow to reach adulthood.

Any two parties to this triad (clutch size, female reproductive investment, and expenditure per progeny) uniquely determine the third; however, forces of natural selection molding each differ substantially. Clutch or litter weight presumably reflects an adult female's best current investment tactic in a given environment at a particular instant in time, whereas expenditure on any given individual progeny is more closely attuned to the average environment encountered by a juvenile. Clutch or litter size is thus the direct result of the interaction between an optimal parental reproductive tactic and an optimal juvenile size (clutch size is simply the ratio of the former divided by the latter).

Two of the lizard species with the highest expenditures per progeny, *Typhlosaurus gariepensis* and *T. lineatus*, almost certainly experience intense competition: (1) these live-bearing, subterranean Kalahari skinks exist at very high population densities, (2) individuals are long-lived with delayed maturity, (3) litter sizes are extremely small (means of 1.0, and 1.5, respectively), and (4) females very likely reproduce only biennially. These two Kalahari fossorial skinks are also both extreme food specialists, eating termites to the virtual exclusion of all other prey. The exceedingly high expenditure per progeny of *Typhlosaurus* may well be necessary to confer newborn animals with competitive ability sufficient to establish themselves in the highly competitive underground environment. Limited evidence indicates that investment per progeny is indeed responsive to, and indicative of, a lizard's competitive environment. Thus, in *Typhlosaurus lineatus*, offspring are significantly heavier (and expenditure per progeny significantly greater) where this species occurs in sympatry with *T. gariepensis* as compared with allopatric populations. Other food-specialized species seem also to encounter intense competition. Among Australian geckos, species with relatively restricted termite diets tend to lay comparatively larger eggs, and hence have higher expenditures per progeny than do those with more catholic diets.

ESCAPE FROM PREDATORS

Tails of many, but by no means all, lizards break off easily (indeed, some species can actually lose their tails voluntarily with minimal external force in a process known as autotomy). Freshly dismembered tails or pieces thereof typically thrash around wildly, attracting a predator's attention while the recent owner quietly slips away unnoticed. Certain small predators, such as the pygmy varanids *Varanus gilleni* and *V. caudolineatus*, actually "harvest" the exceedingly fragile tails of geckos that are too large to subdue intact. Some skinks, including many *Ctenotus*, return to the site where their tail was lost and swallow the remains of their own tail! Few, if any, other vertebrates display auto-amputation and self-cannibalism.

Many such lizards possess special adaptations for tail loss, including weak fracture planes within each tail vertebra, muscular attachments that facilitate autotomy and tail movement after dismemberment, as well as mechanisms for rapidly closing off blood vessels and promoting healing. Losing its tail has surprisingly little effect on a lizard, as individuals often resume basking and foraging within minutes, as if nothing had happened. In such lizard species, of course, tails are quickly regenerated from the stub. Regrown tails are occasionally almost indistinguishable from the original externally, but their internal support structure is cartilaginous rather than bony.

Not all lizard tails are easily broken, however. Whereas most iguanines have fragile tails, their close relatives the agamids generally do not. Tails of varanids and of true chameleons do not break easily either. Lizards with such tough tails usually cannot regenerate a very complete tail if their original should happen to be lost. The evolutionary bases for these differences, sometimes between fairly closely related groups of lizards, are evasive and merit further scrutiny.

Lizard tails have diversified greatly, and they serve a wide variety of other functions for their possessors. Many climbing species, such as the Australian sandridge agamid *Gemmatophora longirostris*, have evolved extraordinarily long tails (three times the snout-vent length), which serve as effective counterbalances. Tail-removal experiments have shown that such long tails also enable lizards to raise their forelegs off the ground and to run on their hind legs alone (bipedality is a faster means of locomotion than tetrapodality). Prehensile tails are used as a fifth leg in climbing by other arboreal lizard species like some geckos (e.g., *Diplodactylus elderi*), and by the true chameleons such as *Chameleo dilepis* of the Kalahari.

In several members of the Australian gekkonid genus *Diplodactylus* (*D. ciliaris*, *D. elderi*, and *D. strophurus*), glandular tails secrete and store a smelly noxious mucous. When disturbed, these lizards squirt out large amounts of sticky odoriferous goo. Surprisingly, tails of these geckos are fragile and easily shed (but quickly regenerated). One night, a small snake, and two geckos, including a *ciliaris*, fell into a pit trap: all were glued tightly together with *ciliaris* goo the next morning. A related Australian desert gecko, *Diplodactylus conspicillatus*, has a nonglandular but very short, stubby bony tail; these nocturnal termite specialists hide in the vertical shafts of abandoned spider holes during the day, and it is thought that they point head downward and use their tails to block off these tunnels. Another Australian desert lizard with a similar yet different tail tactic is the climbing skink *Egernia depressa*. These lizards wedge themselves into tight crevices in mulga tree hollows (and rocks), blocking off the entrance with their strong and very spiny tails. Spinily armored tails are used by numerous other species of lizards in a similar fashion, including the Mexican iguanian *Enyaliosaurus clarki* and the Saharan agamid *Uromastix acanthinurus*.

Members of a bizarre group of Australian geckos (genus *Nephrurus*) possess a unique round knob at the tip of their tails. These large nocturnal lizards eat big prey, including other species of geckos on occasion. Both sexes carry the curious knob, but its function remains a total mystery. Unlike most geckos, their tails are not very fragile. *Nephrurus* will stand their ground, and hiss and lunge with an open mouth in a sort of threat display. At such times, they also tend to arch their tails up over their backs, displaying the vivid white underside (their tails do break off if any pressure is applied).

In many species of lizards (especially among juveniles), tails are brightly colored, and/or very conspicuous, evidently functioning to lure a potential predator's attack away from the more vulnerable, less dispensable parts of the animal. Thus, when approached or followed by a large animal, the zebra-tailed lizard of the western North American deserts, *Callisaurus draconoides*, curls its tail up over its hindquarters and back, exposing the bold black-and-white pattern underneath, and coyly wriggles its tail from side to side. If pursued farther, zebra-tailed lizards resort to extreme speed (estimated at up to 20–30 km/hr) and long zigzag runs. An Australian desert skink, *Ctenotus calurus*, lashes and quivers its bright azure blue tail alongside its body continuously as it forages slowly through the open spaces between plants, and tiny *Morethia butleri* juveniles twitch their bright red tails as they move around in the litter beneath *Eucalyptus* trees.

The potential of tail break frequency as an index to the intensity of predation on lizard populations was noted long ago by the legendary J. B. S. Haldane, and has since been used as a sort of bioassay to attempt to estimate the amount of predation, although there are some problems and limitations with the procedure. Efficient predators that leave no surviving prey obviously will not produce broken tails, but nevertheless may exert substantial predation pressures; broken and regenerated tails may therefore reflect lizard escape ability or predator inefficiency better than intensity of predation. In western North America, predator densities increase from north to south. Correlated with this latitudinal increase in predation, frequencies of broken and regenerated tails are higher at southern sites than at northern localities among four of the five widely distributed lizard species. In the well-studied desert whiptail species *Cnemidophorus tigris*, the frequency of broken tails decreases with latitude; moreover, diversity of predator escape behaviors utilized among members of various populations of other species of *Cnemidophorus* also increases with the frequency of broken and regenerated tails. A greater variety of escape tactics, a form of behavioral "aspect diversity," presumably reduces the ease with which predators can capture lizard prey.

A nocturnal Australian skink, *Eremiascincus richardsoni*, very probably mimics the large centipede *Scolpendra mortisans*. Both are nocturnal, both frequent burrows, both are strongly banded with glossy yellow and black, and both have a reddish head. Of course, the centipede is poisonous, with venomous claws on each of its many legs as well as a toxic bite, whereas the skinks are quite defenseless. I have been told that, if a centipede ever begins to run across your bare skin, you should not try to sweep it off with your hand against the direction it is moving, as that will only assure that its poisonous claws will dig into your flesh. You can, apparently, sweep one off in the same direction that it is moving without getting poisoned. Think, before you react. Reflexes can get you into trouble!

Notes to Chapter 4

1. Interestingly, no North American desert lizard has evolved into a scorpion specialist, even though these large arachnids are moderately plentiful. Some snakes, such as *Chilomeniscus* and *Chionactis*, do prey on scorpions in North American deserts.

2. Due to their very short duration, these bursts of high food availability, with their associated extensive dietary overlap, have only a trivial impact on overall utilization patterns.

3. One Namib Desert lacertid species, *Aporosaura anchietae*, actually switches from sitting and waiting for wind-blown seeds when winds are blowing to foraging widely for insect prey when winds are calm.

HISTORY

AUSTRALIA IS CALLED THE ISLAND CONTINENT FOR GOOD reason—it has long been isolated from other continents. Unlike Eurasia, the Americas, or even Africa, only relatively recently has Australia been subjected to invasions from outside via New Guinea. During the late Paleozoic era, long before humans, even before placental mammals, 230 million years ago during the beginnings of the age of dinosaurs, Australia was part of a great landmass known as Pangaea, which consisted of all the continents connected together. A large block known as Laurasia, which later separated into North America and Eurasia, soon broke off, and began drifting north. The remaining southern landmass, known as Gondwanaland, consisted of the three southern continents, Africa, South America, and Australia, plus the tectonic plate destined to become India, all of which remained connected to Antarctica. Earth was much warmer then, and Gondwanaland was populated with dinosaurs.

During the Mesozoic, about 180 million years ago, Gondwana began to fragment into several tectonic plates. India broke off and sailed rapidly—by geological standards—northward like a giant Noah's ark, carrying its flora and fauna with it, where its collision with Eurasia formed the Himalayas.[1] South America plus Africa, remaining connected to each other, began to pull away from Australia-Antarctica; finally, about 100 myBP, Africa broke free and began to drift northward. By the late Mesozoic (70 million years ago), the Indian plate along with its biota was midway across the ocean that later became known as the Indian Ocean. South America, Australia, and Antarctica remained attached together until the early Cenozoic, sharing marsupials. About 50 million years ago, Australia finally broke off and began its own slow drift northward. Australia entered the tropics about 20 myBP, still remaining fairly wet. Aridification of Australia began about 10–15 myBP, as forests gave way first to grasslands and then to deserts. The Australian continent has been more or less in its present position for the last several million years. Imagine the effects of changing climates on plants and animals as tectonic plates and continents drift through different latitudes! As Australia continues to move toward the equator, its climate will gradually become wetter and increasingly more and more tropical.

Certain types of rocks, particularly basalts, retain a magnetic "memory" of the latitude in which they were solidified. Such paleomagnetic evidence allows mapping of the past position of the North Pole. (An intriguing but still unexplained phenomenon has been discovered: magnetic polarity reversed several times during geological time, with the last reversal about 700,000 years ago.) Recent rocks from different locations coincide in pinpointing the pole's position, but paleomagnetic records from older rocks from different localities are in discord. These discrepancies strongly suggest that the continents have moved with respect to one another. The continents are formed of light "plates" of siliceous, largely granitic, rocks about thirty kilometers thick, which in turn float on heavier mantlelike basaltic blocks. The ocean floors are composed of a relatively thin altered top of the earth's mantle. A mountain range on the sea floor in the mid-Atlantic has recently been mapped, and this ridge represents a region of upwelling of the mantle. Under this interpretation, as the upwelling proceeds, sea floors spread, and continents move apart. The positions of paleomagnetic anomalies (polarity reversals) in the sea floor allow geologists to calculate the velocity of lateral motion of the ocean floors, which correspond to comparable estimates for the landmasses. Thus, modern theory holds that, except for the Pacific (which is shrinking), oceans are growing, with very young ocean floors in mid-ocean, and progressively older floors toward the continents. Other evidence, such as the apparent ages of islands and the depths of sediments, nicely corroborates this conclusion.

There is also ample biogeographical evidence for continental drift. For example, certain very ancient groups of plants, freshwater lungfishes, amphibians, and insects that had arisen and spread before the breakup of the continents now occur on several continents, whereas many other more recently evolved groups of animals, such as mammals and birds, are restricted to particular biogeographic regions. Cold-adapted fossil plants (*Glossopteris*) are found from the Triassic of South America, Australia, Africa, and Antarctica. Similarly, present day remnants of southern beech forests (*Nothofagus*) are found in southern Chile, Australia, and Tasmania, and occur as fossil pollens in Antarctica.

Classical biogeography assumed some permanence in the locations of continents. As a result, interpretations of faunal similarities between them often relied on hypothetical mechanisms of transport from one continent to another, such as improbable land bridges or "rafting" of organisms across water gaps. Such long-distance dispersal events are exceedingly improbable, although they have clearly occurred from time to time. Land tortoises had to have rafted to remote volcanic islands such as the Galapagos and Aldabra. Skinks and geckos must be adept at dispersal, for they are present on most Pacific islands, even quite remote ones. Similarly, cattle egrets made a successful trans-Atlantic crossing from Africa to South America without human assistance during recorded history late in the eighteenth century. Much of classical biogeography is still being reinterpreted in light of the new discovery that the continents are drifting.

One consequence of the long isolation of Australia was that marsupials flourished there. Due to the paucity of fossils and gaps in the paleontological record, no one can say for certain where any given taxon arose and first evolved, although biogeographers cannot resist speculating about the locations of origins of major groups. To date, Australia has a fairly limited ancient fossil record. An exception is the 120-million-year-old fossil platypus from Lightning Ridge, Queensland. New discoveries are still being made. The oldest Aussie marsupials date from only 23 myBP (million years before present), long after Australia was separated from the other elements of Gondwana. Older marsupial fossils are known from Europe, North America, South America, and Antarctica. The oldest known putative marsupial fossil, *Holoclemensia texana*, 120 myBP, is from Texas! (*Holoclemensia* might not be a genuine marsupial at all.) Presumably, marsupials somehow reached Australia about 100 myBP, before it became completely separated from Antarctica. For eons, South America and Australia were similarly isolated, both supporting a rich adaptive radiation of marsupials (placentals had apparently replaced marsupials elsewhere). A few placentals did manage to reach South America during the Cenozoic, but none were able to reach Australia until the Pleistocene epoch. When the Isthmus of Panama arose about 3 myBP, North America and South America became connected for the first time, and there was a massive reciprocal exchange of biotic elements, termed the great American biotic interchange. Many, though not all, Neotropical marsupials went extinct as the Nearctic placentals invaded South America. A few Neotropical forms, such as the opossum, armadillo, and porcupine, were able to invade North America. But, marsupials continued to thrive in Australia due to its isolation.

Some students of lizard biogeography and phylogeny have argued that all families except the agamids are of Gondwanan origin (Estes 1983). Some of the oldest lepidosaur fossils are from Australia (Molnar 1985). The paliguanid *Kudnu mackinleyi*, among the oldest and most primitive of all lizards, is thought to be ancestral to all later squamates (lizards and snakes). Paliguanids are known only from Australia and South Africa, suggesting that lizards arose in Gondwanaland. Other workers (Greer 1989) have asserted that four of the five families of lizards found in Australia arose in the Northern Hemisphere and subsequently dispersed to Australia, the exception being the snakelike pygopodids, which are thought to have arisen within Australia from diplodactyline geckos (which themselves probably evolved from another gekkonid lineage within Australia). In any case, the four lizard lineages that did reach Australia underwent extensive adaptive radiations on the island continent, with some, such as the varanids, becoming more speciose there than they are today in their probable source areas.

Aboriginal humans arrived in Australia relatively recently in geological time, only about 50,000 to 120,000 years ago. Aborigines have thus been on the island continent for less than 0.01 percent of its geological history. More recently, probably within the past 5,000 years, Aborigines probably introduced the first carnivorous placental mammal, the dingo. Introduction of the dingo presumably caused the recent extinction of a large doglike predator, the thylacine (these marsupials went extinct on the Australian mainland only about 8,000 years ago, but persisted in Tasmania until the 1930s, where they became known as the Tasmanian tiger or wolf). It remains harder to guess where Australian Aborigines came from than when they arrived (there were probably several immigrations).

During the Pleistocene, Australia was much wetter and supported a fauna of large animals (known as a megafauna) such as the Diprotodon marsupials, most of which have since gone extinct, and are known only from fossils. One of the most interesting Pleistocene fossils is the gigantic varanid lizard *Megalania prisca*, a beast estimated to have reached a total length of nearly ten meters. A reconstruction of the skeleton of *Megalania* is on display in the National Museum. The Sydney Museum has an enormous life-sized magnificent model of the intact lizard. Being contemporary with humans, in all probability *Megalania* ate *Homo*, more than once. *Megalania* teeth were over two centimeters long, curved, with the rear edge serrated for cutting and tearing the skin and flesh of its prey.

Discovered by the Dutch, and first known as New Holland, Australia was the last continent to be settled by Europeans, and then it was settled in a rather curious way as a British penal colony, a mere two centuries ago. Thousands of petty thieves as well as some hardened criminals received the sentence of "transportation," which meant permanent banishment from the beloved British Isles. Prisoners wore uniforms marked Prisoners of Mother England (the origin of the word "pome" or "pom") while working off their sentences (some in chains), and many became free men and women. The British quickly settled the edges of the continent to prevent other countries from laying any claim to it. As noted earlier, Aborigines have dwelled in Australia for less than 0.01 percent of the island continent's existence. White Europeans settled in 1788 and have been present for only one five-hundredth of that time, but have made incredibly drastic changes during that brief two-century timespan. One year after white settlement, a smallpox epidemic killed off most of the Aborigines around Sydney. During the first century of European settlement, from 1788 to 1888, a continent that had never known a hoofed animal during the past 200 million years suddenly found itself with over a million sheep, goats, cows, and horses. Needless to say, the impact of all those hooves and hungry mouths in a mere one hundred years was enormous. Some have speculated that bush flies must have been much less abundant before the introduction of domestic stock, and the consequent vast amount of feces. During the second century of European occupation, from 1888 to 1988, changes have been even more drastic.

Large regions of central Australia remained unexplored until the middle to late 1800s. Many expected to find a great inland sea. Quite a few men perished undertaking the perilous exploration of the waterless interior, whereas a number of others just barely squeaked through with their lives. Edward Eyre managed the first overland crossing from South Australia to Western Australia in 1840, traveling along the southern coast, and losing several men. In 1844–1845, Captain Charles Sturt reconnoitered South Australia's stony deserts and salt lake country as well as the southern fringe of the Simpson Desert. Ludwig Leichardt's entire expedition vanished without a trace somewhere in central Australia in 1847. In 1860, John Stuart discovered a north-south route from Adelaide to Darwin, which later became the telegraph line. Only one man, John King, survived the (Robert O'Hara) Burke and (William John) Wills Expedition, which made a famous north-south crossing from Adelaide to the Gulf of Carpentaria in 1860–1861. Colonel Peter Egerton Warburton and his small party of men just barely managed to cross the Great Sandy Desert from Alice Springs to Roebourne in 1872, after losing all but two camels and coming perilously close to dying along the way. The brave British explorer Ernest Giles finally succeeded in making an east-west crossing through the arid center in 1874, after several abortive attempts, including one in which he came very close to dying. Giles lost an inept assistant he sent for help on their only surviving horse (Giles managed to walk out on foot, whereas Gibson, after whom the Gibson Desert is named, rode, got lost, and perished).

Until the 1850s, Australia had difficulty attracting voluntary immigrants, but the discovery of extensive fields of alluvial gold changed that overnight, and led to a rapid doubling, and then an almost immediate redoubling, of the human population, mostly young males in their prime. Men from all around the world migrated to Australia seeking their fortunes. For the first century or so, there was a serious shortage of females in most of Australia. Efforts were made to attract single women immigrants by offering them cheap or free passage. Men lived and worked in the outback for years on end without even seeing a white woman. An intense sense of male-male camaraderie and loyalty developed between pairs of men who had to rely on one another in life-and-death situations. Members of such a pair referred to one another as "mates." It was not uncommon for one member of a pair to carry the other hundreds of kilometers when sickness or injuries dictated. Today many Aussie males are sexual chauvinists, referring to women as "sheilas." The hard, womanless life faced by men in the outback, plus the legacy of the British lower classes, probably explains why Aussie men congregate in pubs and are such big beer drinkers, not to mention being devoted "skimpy" fans.

During the first 150 years of its existence, Australia was under exceedingly strong, almost stifling, influence from Great Britain. Britain did not always treat its colonies well: incredibly, in the 1940s, without even telling the Aussie public, the British secretly tested atomic bombs north of Ooldea at Maralinga in the remote Great Victoria Desert of South Australia! In the recent effort to distance themselves from Great Britain, but remaining ever loyal to the royalty, some Australians refer to the British Queen as the "Queen of Australia." After the Second World War, the influence of the United States was heightened. Nowadays, Australia is threatened with becoming a colony of Japan.

The island continent has been repeatedly assaulted by invasions from exotic plants and animals, often deliberately by displaced Europeans nostalgic for creatures that remind them of "home." So-called acclimatization societies imported numerous European plants, and some animals. Noxious plants, such as prickly pear cactus and many others, were introduced both accidentally and deliberately. Animals such as cats and camels became feral (today Australia harbors the world's largest and healthiest population of Arabian camels, whence they are now exported back to Arabia).

One of the worst of these ecocatastrophes occurred in 1859, when a dozen pairs of European rabbits (*Oryctolagus cuniculus*) were imported and released into the wild by Thomas Austin at Geelong, Victoria. (Foxes had already been introduced earlier but had died out—unfortunately, they were reintroduced in the 1860s, in part to help control the rabbits when they "took.") Rabbits being rabbits, they bred like rabbits and multiplied rapidly. Over 20,000 rabbits were killed on a single hunt a decade later.

In the absence of natural enemies and pathogens, the rabbit population burgeoned and quickly spread northward, but primarily westward. Vast areas were decimated by hordes of hungry rabbits. Ground cover was destroyed. Reports of koalas from inland areas being well outside their geographic range proved to be starving rabbits desperately climbing sloping trees trying to get at something green to eat! An enormous area of prime pastoral land was ruined for domestic stock. Fodder was gone. Sheep, cattle, and horses died both from starvation and from breaking their legs falling through into rabbit warrens. Water holes were deliberately poisoned, leaving millions of rabbit corpses. Rabbits were chased into corrals and clubbed to death. When word of this rabbit plague in eastern Australia reached the pastoralists in Western Australia, the latter decided to have no part of it and undertook to build rabbit-proof fences (RPFs) across the arid heart of Australia. This was truly a superhuman effort in the late 1800s. Three RPFs were erected across the waterless desert interior, all the way from the Indian Ocean in the north to the Great Australian Bight in the south. Heavy-gauge, tight-meshed galvanized chicken wire was buried half a meter underground and extended aboveground a couple of meters. Men were hired as fence tenders, and with camels, they patrolled up and down the fences, keeping them in good repair. Some say that the rabbits got past before the fences were closed, but we will never know for certain.

One, possibly apocryphal, eyewitness account of a fence tender is worth recounting simply because it is such a good story. As he was leading his camel carrying supplies down the western side of one of the rabbit-proof fences, the fence tender noticed a cloud of dust on the eastern horizon that was quickly coming closer. There wasn't enough wind for willy willies, and it soon became apparent that the dust was being made by thousands upon thousands of migrating rabbits, beating westward toward the RPF. As he watched, the first rabbits collided with the fence and piled into it. These were quickly followed by more rabbits, which pressed against the first wave to form a wall of crushed rabbits—within minutes, the rabbit tidal wave piled up into a ramp of rabbit bodies, and live rabbits poured up, and spilled right over the top of the "rabbit-proof" fence! So the "best-laid plans of men" failed utterly, and by 1904 rabbits had reached the west coast of Australia. Eventually, the geographical range of rabbits in Australia stabilized, covering the southern two-thirds of the continent (having evolved in the Northern Temperate Zone, they were unable to invade tropical Australia). By providing food for foxes, rabbits may have indirectly enhanced the spread of foxes, as well as increased fox populations, and hence indirectly facilitated predation on native marsupials. Many consider the fox to be the real culprit in the extinctions of mid-sized marsupials.

Over the next half century, beleaguered Aussies continued their poisoning and trapping of rabbits, as well as organizing rabbit-clubbing efforts around water holes during droughts, killing hundreds of thousands of rabbits, but the rabbits simply bred right back up to enormous numbers. Finally, during the late 1940s, a biological-control swat team was set up, and it began searching for a control pathogen. A carcinogenic myxoma virus—which produces a mild nonlethal disease in its natural host, the South American cottontail rabbit *Sylvilagus brasilensis*—was identified that was exceedingly virulent in *Oryctolagus*. In 1950, this virus was introduced as a biological control agent in Australia in an effort to eradicate the European rabbit *Oryctolagus cuniculus*. Fleas and mosquitos transmit the virus between infected rabbits. Initially, the virus caused better than a 99-percent kill among infected rabbits. Of course, selection was intense for increased resistance among rabbits. Even so, a less virulent strain of myxoma virus rapidly became established in the field. Apparently, the exceedingly virulent strain often killed its host outright even before it could be transmitted to other rabbits, whereas less virulent strains were more likely to persist long enough to be passed on to other hosts. Reduced virulence evolved in this situation. But in others, such as with influenzas, a parasite finds itself engaged in a race against its host's immune response, and natural selection may actually favor the evolution of increased virulence. Aussie scientists today are working on development of viral-borne genetic agents for the sterilization of rabbits and foxes.

Another major feat of engineering was the completion of an incredible 600-km aqueduct from Perth to Kalgoorlie in 1903. Miners suffered great deprivations from the lack of reliable water before the construction of this aquifer. Many people actually made their living distilling saline water and selling fresh water by the gallon. Indeed, by bringing a reliable water supply to the goldfields region, this pipe allowed the subsequent settlement and inhabitation of the area. Without the Kalgoorlie aqueduct, I could never have done my research. Some Aussie politicians now favor a massive Texas-style water plan to move "excess" water from the Kimberley in northern Western Australia to the south.

Virtually all the birds in Perth are native species, such as lorikeets, Twenty-eight Parrots, Black Cockatoos, Willie Wagtails, various species of honeyeaters, and magpies. An exception introduced from eastern Australia, kookaburras laugh from tall trees around King's Park, an extensive area of natural bushland in the center of the city. It is no accident that there are still no English sparrows or starlings in Western Australia (even though they do occur in the east). A state agency that acts as the starling patrol answers a hot line and responds to reports of sightings of these birds anywhere along the trans-line (the east-west railroad line across Australia) or the Nullarbor Plain. Its agents are the only people in Australia who have been authorized to have silencers on their guns. (Without a silencer, you get only one bird in a flock, but with a silencer, you can shoot all of them!) If someone reports a sighting of three starlings, an agent promptly appears and doesn't depart until he or she has eliminated all three of them.

Note to Chapter 5

1. Massive movements of the continents themselves were first suggested by F. B. Taylor in 1910, although his bold hypothesis was not widely accepted. Taylor speculated that our moon was captured by the earth, causing an increase in the speed of rotation, which in turn "threw" the continents away from the poles and toward the equator by centrifugal forces. He also suggested, almost certainly correctly, that the Himalayan mountains were formed by the collision of two tectonic plates. However, other scientists, such as Alfred Wegener, are usually credited with the idea of continental drift.

LOST

"OUTBACK" AUSTRALIA REFERS TO THE AREAS BEYOND the last outposts of civilization, the last small towns and pastoral stations. This much-feared region is sometimes referred to as the "land of the never never" or the "place where dead men lie." Many Australians are uncomfortable in the bush, and somewhat obsessed with the idea of death by thirst in the red desert. Compared with many other places, the Australian outback is fairly benign. The only really dangerous animals are a few poisonous snakes (and, potentially, feral camels). In the goldfields, open mine shafts constitute a danger. The outback demands respect, as it can be a dangerous place because of its lack of water and extreme isolation. You cannot expect anyone to wander by to help you. Total self-sufficiency is required. Venture deeply into the outback only when prepared for any exigency, and even then at your own risk and with a certain amount of trepidation. Carry enough food, fuel, and water to last several weeks. Take good care of your vehicle, and know it, for it is your life-support system. Also, take as many spare parts for your vehicle as possible, a manual, plus a complete tool kit. Know how to repair virtually anything that might go wrong. It's wise to have an extra spare tire, and a two-battery system, with one always in reserve. Matilda was great in the event of battery failure for she had an old-fashioned hand-crank backup starter! However, Katy's diesel engine could not be started without a charged battery.

Even with all these precautions, a two-way radio is an essential insurance policy. To cope with the vast distances and isolation of the outback, the Royal Flying Doctor Service (RFDS) maintains a regular radio schedule, continually monitoring certain frequencies. The RFDS also maintains planes, and has skilled bush pilots and medical doctors standing by ready to attend to medical emergencies anywhere, anytime. Just knowing that the RFDS is there is a real comfort to everyone in the outback. I still have my appendix. Once I had a kidney stone, which was exceedingly painful. Alone in the outback, I sometimes worry about what I would do in the event of a serious illness or injury. I suppose I would have no choice but to dope myself up with whatever painkiller I could find, and do my best to drive myself out! Also, if I were so bad off that I couldn't even drive, my transceiver has an emergency signal switch that sends out a continuous directional alarm like an airplane beacon station (constantly monitored by the RFDS). I would press this button only as I was passing out, fully expecting to die.

Cautious people will not even venture into the outback unless they can go in trains of two or more vehicles. Others rely on regular radio contacts. Another standard procedure is to leave word with someone at the last place before departure into the outback that one will emerge on the other side within some specified time period, at which time safe arrival is announced. Search-and-rescue parties are sent out if scheduled radio contacts are not made. Because I could not adhere to any such firm schedule, I had to do things somewhat differently. Relying on my own self-sufficiency, I went out alone and did not make regular radio contact, but counted on my transceiver as my ace of trump, an emergency backup system to be used when all else failed. I always carry ample supplies of food, fuel, and water, and I become nervous when supplies fall below about half.

On our first trip deep into the Great Victoria Desert, I topped up our fuel and water in Kalgoorlie, and we drove out the road along the trans-line. At a railway stop called Rawlinna, we looked for a track heading north into the desert. On the maps, this north-south track crossed over an east-west track several hundred kilometers to the north at a point labeled "Neale Junction," and then continued on several hundred kilometers farther north to Warburton, a distant Aboriginal settlement well into the Gibson Desert (Figure 7). Because the area immediately around Rawlinna on the Nullarbor Plain is covered by a maze of rabbit hunters' tracks, we could not, however,

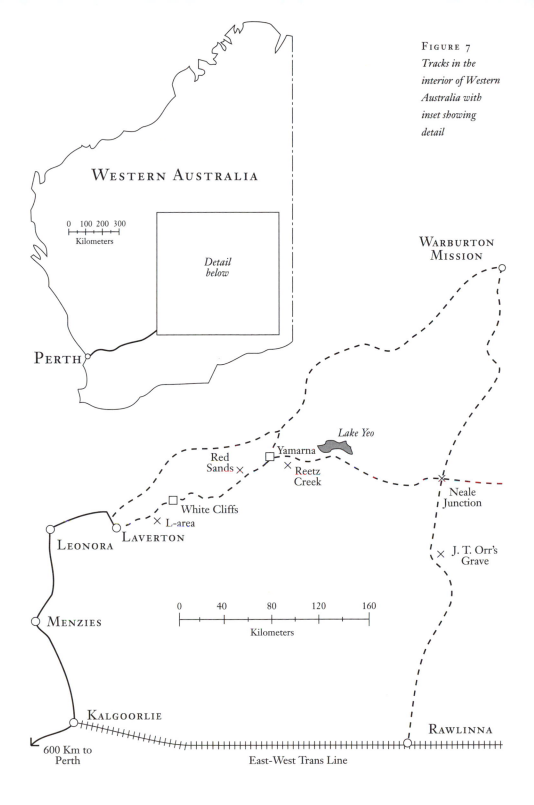

FIGURE 7
*Tracks in the
interior of Western
Australia with
inset showing
detail*

WESTERN AUSTRALIA

0 100 200 300
Kilometers

*Detail
below*

PERTH

WARBURTON
MISSION

Lake Yeo

Red
Sands ✕

□ Yamarna
✕ Reetz
Creek

Neale
Junction

□
White Cliffs
✕ L-area

LEONORA LAVERTON

✕ J. T. Orr's
Grave

0   40   80   120   160
Kilometers

MENZIES

KALGOORLIE

600 Km to
Perth

East-West Trans Line

RAWLINNA

locate the major north-south track into the desert. We drove around for half a day, wasting precious fuel, trying to find the track but failed. Finally, the next day, in desperation, we drove back into Rawlinna and looked about for someone from whom to ask directions. Upon finding the station master's wife, I asked for directions to the Warburton track. Carefully sizing us up and looking us over, she pointed to a track and said to follow it for about forty kilometers until we came to a windmill at Seemore Downs, which was very near the track we wanted, and to ask for further directions there. We soon found the little-traveled road, which was the only properly graded track in the area (other than the trans-line road itself), and the only one that ran straight as an arrow almost due north (Figure 7).

As we drove along toward Neale Junction, the skeletons of long-dead trees, sun-bleached bone white, sparkled amidst the dark green living trees. For mile after pristine mile, we went along this untraveled track, deeper and deeper into the desert wilderness, feeling like real explorers, fantasizing about finding something really phenomenal, such as a rare marsupial, or even one long thought to be extinct. We even considered the possibility of finding a thylacine. One would be stupid not to be somewhat apprehensive, going so far into a real no-man's-land.

At our first camp on the southern fringe of the desert in a zone of myall vegetation, we found some very interesting geckos that we hadn't previously encountered. The next day we entered and drove all day through pristine spinifex sandy desert country, solemnly passing J. T. Orr's (R. I. P.) grave along the way. At dusk, we pulled about ten meters off the track to camp about twenty-seven kilometers south of Neale Junction. Geckoing was quite good that night, too. Diurnal lizarding was outstanding the next day, so we stayed put right there alongside the track for nearly a week (this site became my most remote study area). After a few more days, huge clouds began to billow up. When it began to look like serious rain was inevitable, we decided that it would be prudent to leave before we got stranded by bogs.

One cannot help but be amused by the absurdity of Neale Junction itself, which is simply a forlorn place in the middle of nowhere where two once-bulldozed and graded tracks happen to cross. Right in the center of the "intersection," surrounded by a huge grader tire painted white was an aluminum ("alumin*i*um" down under) plaque stamped out by the intrepid road builder Len Beadell a few years earlier, giving

Helen leaves a note at Neale Junction (1967).

his estimate (made by shooting the stars with a sextant) of the exact latitude and longitude. There was also a steel post to which a couple of whitewashed large welder's gloves were wired, along with a coffee jar. The jar contained notes left by anyone and everyone who had ever been through Neale Junction (really no small accomplishment in itself). Most simply gave names and dates, but a few attempted humorous remarks such as "It's high time the Neale Junction Shire Council installed traffic lights here, or at least Stop signs!" Helen left our own innocuous little note in the bottle saying "Eric and Helen

Pianka, Dept. Zoology, Univ. of W. A., Lizard hunters. 19 Jan. 1967. 12.55 P.M. Heading to Laverton."

It soon began to rain as we headed west toward Laverton, and that night it poured to the point that I began to fear that we might not be able to get out. I even set up a tarp and collected rainwater for drinking as a precaution. (A tropical monsoon, "Elsie," was moving inland—this storm dropped as much as 300 mm of precipitation in some places, turning much of inland Australia into a bog.) As we approached the tiny outback town of Laverton for the first time, we stopped, and heard noises that sounded like dozens of model airplane engines—it turned out to be a breeding colony of desert frogs (*Cyclorana*),[1] with many males chorusing to attract females in a pond (previously, the "road"). We did, however, reach the sealed road to Kalgoorlie just before the dirt tracks became entirely impassable.

Totally unbeknownst to us, the Rawlinna station master's wife radioed Warburton soon after we passed through, telling them that a young couple was on their way northward in a short wheelbased Land Rover without adequate supplies of food or water (in this appraisal, she was quite incorrect—Mat was a long wheelbase, and we were quite well equipped). Although we had asked for directions to the Warburton track, we had never had any intention of driving all the way through to Warburton, but had always intended to turn west at Neale Junction, and to come out of the desert at Laverton. To our intense chagrin, we had become the objects of an ill-founded search-and-rescue mission as well as front-page news. Australian newspapers have a flair for the sensational: on our return, we found that papers with our "story" had been sold under a large placard that said DESERT MYSTERY DEEPENS in red letters 75 mm high.

I first learned of all this almost two weeks later while routinely refilling our fuel tanks in the rain at a petrol station in Kalgoorlie on our way back to Perth. An Aussie woman came up to me and said, "You the one whot was lost?" To which I replied, "No, ma'am, I haven't been lost." Then she said, "That's funny, beard and," glancing at my neck, "a snake in a test tube around your neck, and all." To take active body temperatures of lizards, I always carry a small thermometer wrapped in a pipe cleaner in a plastic tube hanging around my neck. I knew at once that she must in fact be referring to a description of me, and so went straight to the police station to declare myself "found." Upon our return to Perth, we collected the following newspaper clippings reporting our misadventure:

DAILY NEWS,
FRIDAY, JANUARY 20, 1967, PAGE 2:

DESERT SEARCH FOR COUPLE MISSING IN CAR

Police are searching for a mystery couple missing in near century temperatures north-east of Kalgoorlie.

They are looking for a man about 23 and a girl about 20, believed to be in a vehicle with little water and only a couple of blankets.

The couple were last seen eight days ago heading north through the central desert country on a track to Warburton Range.

A Government dogger in the area followed their tracks for 180 miles but lost them.

Police do not know who the couple are but are alarmed because of the possibilities of them being in serious trouble without fuel or water.

DAILY NEWS,
FRIDAY, JANUARY 20, 1967, PAGE 3:

SEARCH FOR TWO MISSING IN DESERT

Police are searching for a mystery couple missing in near century temperatures north-east of Kalgoorlie.

They are looking for a man about 23 and a girl about 20, believed to be in a vehicle with little water and only a couple of blankets.

The couple were last seen eight days ago heading north through the central desert country on a track to Warburton Ranges.

A Government dogger followed their tracks for 130 miles but lost them.

Police do not know who the couple are but are alarmed because of the possibilities of them being in serious trouble without fuel or water.

Two days ago the station master at Rawlinna, on the trans-continental railway, reported that a young man and woman had left there on January 12.

He did not know who they were but said the man had a red beard and had a snake in a test tube hanging around his neck.

They were in a short wheelbase Landrover which does not carry much fuel.

They asked directions to Seemore Downs station, about 30 miles north. They arrived at the station homestead that night.

Station people put them on the Old Military road to Warburton Ranges.

Inspector W. Clarey, of Kalgoorlie, said there are hundreds of tracks in the area.

Police have made exhaustive inquiries to find out who the people are but have not obtained any further information.

By radio government dogger Brown said he had picked up Landrover tracks and had followed them for 130 miles north of Seemore Downs into desert country.

Inspector Clarey asked him to go north to Neal Junction and report back.

Another party has left Warburton Ranges Mission to go south to Neal Junction.

It is about 600 miles by road from Rawlinna to the Warburton Ranges Mission.

Temperatures have been consistently near the century mark for the past week in the area but thunderstorms brought some rain today.

WEST AUSTRALIAN,
SATURDAY, JANUARY 21, 1967, PAGE 2:

TWO MISSING IN DESOLATE INLAND BUSH COUNTRY

Kalgoorlie, Fri: A four-wheel-drive vehicle carrying two young people is missing in desolate country north of Rawlinna, on the trans-Australia railway.

The couple, a man and a woman, were last seen at Seemore Downs station, about 50 miles north of Rawlinna, on Tuesday morning.

The man is about 23, with a red beard, and is carrying a snake in a test tube tied around his neck. The woman is about 20.

A government dogger, Mr. W. Brown, found tracks believed to have been made by the couple's vehicle on an old defence track leading north to the Warburton Ranges native mission.

Mr. Brown will leave Seemore Downs tomorrow morning to follow the track in search of the couple.

Another search vehicle will leave the Warburton Ranges and travel south along the defence track. The missing pair are believed to have good supplies of food and water.

The area is marked by many small tracks used mainly by doggers and police fear that the couple may have turned on to one of these.

The police said today that an air-search might be instituted and all outposts had been put on the alert to watch for the couple.

WEEKEND NEWS,
SATURDAY, JANUARY 21, 1967, PAGE 1:

SEARCHERS FIND MESSAGE

A simple message in a bottle on a post in desert country has halted a search for a young couple believed missing north of the Nullarbor Plain.

It was found by searchers who bounced their way for 250 miles over a rough track looking for them.

The note indicated that the man and woman, last heard of nine days ago, were safe.

Instead of heading towards Warburton Mission they apparently are travelling slowly along a track towards Laverton, collecting reptile specimens.

The couple whom police feared might have broken down and been in difficulties in the Great Victoria Desert are Eric and Helen Pianka.

The Warburton search party reached Neale Junction in the desert today.

It found the message in a bottle used as a desert mail box at the junction.

It read: "Eric and Helen Pianka, Department of Geology, University of WA. Lizard hunters. 19/1/67, 12.55 p.m. Heading to Laverton."

[Professor Waring of the WA University Zoology Department, said today: "They are visiting American zoologists associated with Princeton University. Dr. Pianka and his wife have been in Australia since last August. I believe they are not inexperienced in this type of country but I don't think they know that precise area."]

It has taken the couple since January 12, when they left Seemore Downs station, to travel the 250 miles to Neale Junction.

The Sunday Times,
Jan. 22, 1967, page 3:

'MISSING' COUPLE UNAWARE OF ANY SEARCH

A young couple hunting snakes and lizards north-east of Kalgoorlie are unaware they have sparked off a widespread police search.

The couple, Eric and Helen Pianka, both from the University of Western Australia's Department of Geology, were last seen nine days ago heading north through the central desert on a track to Warburton Ranges. Police at Kalgoorlie are in daily contact with the Warburton Ranges Mission.

When Dr. and Mrs. Pianka failed to arrive at the mission on Thursday, police organised a search for them.

But yesterday, two searchers, Mr. Dick Hawthorn and Mr. Mick Sawyer, found a bottle containing a note at Neales Junction— between Laverton and Warburton Ranges.

Recalled

The note, written at 12.55 pm on Thursday, said the couple were heading for Laverton.

Police have recalled the government dogger, Mr. W. Brown, who followed the couple's tracks for 130 miles but lost them.

Sgt. A. Cole, of the Kalgoorlie Police, said last night that Mr. Hawthorn and Mr. Sawyer would try and catch up with the couple.

They would report their progress on the Royal Flying Doctor Service radio network.

Sgt. Cole said it was obvious Dr. and Mrs. Pianka had decided not to continue on to the Warburton Ranges Mission.

They seemed to be returning to Laverton.

Sgt. Cole said they would be interviewed by police on their arrival.

Dr. Pianka and his wife are visiting American zoologists associated with Princeton University.

They have been in Australia since last August.

WEST AUSTRALIAN,
MONDAY, JANUARY 23, 1967, PAGE 14:

AMERICAN PAIR SAFE

Two Americans, who were believed to be missing in desolate country north of Rawlinna on the trans-Australia railway, arrived in Kalgoorlie on Saturday night unaware that a search party had been looking for them.

They are Dr. E. Pianka and his wife Helen, who reported to the Kalgoorlie police after having been told they were thought to be missing.

The search had been called off on Saturday morning after a search party found a note the couple had left at Neale Junction, about 300 miles from Rawlinna.

WEST AUSTRALIAN,
TUESDAY, JANUARY 24, 1967, PAGE 8:

COUPLE ON TRACK WERE NOT LOST

Two Americans, Dr Eric Pianka and his wife Helen, who had been thought lost north of Rawlinna on the track leading to the Warburton Ranges, have arrived in Perth.

Dr Pianka is in W.A. on a post-doctorate research fellowship from Princeton University, New Jersey, U.S.A.

He is an experienced field-worker. He spent several years collecting material for his doctorate in which he specialised in lizard ecology.

He and his wife, a biologist holding a doctorate, have spent most of their time in the outback since they arrived in Australia in August.

No Danger

Dr Pianka said they were not in danger during their latest trip.

They had 50 gallons of fuel, 40 gallons of water, 50 cans of beer and 150 cans of cool drink.

They carried a two-way radio with a 35ft. aerial and about $100 worth of spare parts for their four-wheel drive vehicle.

He described as nonsense a rumour that he carried a snake in a test tube tied round his neck.

He carried a thermometer, wrapped in a pipe-cleaner in a little plastic tube hung round his neck.

He used the thermometer to measure the temperature of the lizards he found.

Dr Pianka said they had not intended to go to the Warburton Ranges; they had merely asked the station master at Rawlinna how they could find the Warburton track.

They stayed about a week just south of Neal Junction and did not leave the track.

At Neal Junction they had written the note which was found by searchers.

Dr Pianka said many people left notes in a tin tied to a post at this point.

They were in Perth to refit their vehicle before going into the bush south of Sandstone in about a week.

Search for two missing in desert

POLICE are searching for a mystery couple missing in near century temperatures north-east of Kalgoorlie.

They are looking for a man about 23 and a girl about 20, believed to be in a vehicle with little...

A young couple hunting snakes and lizards north-east of Kalgoor-

2 Missing In Desolate Inland Bush Country

KALGOORLIE, Fri: A four-wheel-drive vehicle carrying two young people is missing in desolate country north of Rawlinna, on the trans-Australia railway.

The couple, a man and a woman, were last seen at Seemore Downs station, about 50 miles north of Rawlinna, on Tuesday morning.

The man is about 23, with a red beard, and is carrying Ranges native mission.

Mr Brown will leave Seemore Downs tomorrow morning to follow the track in search of the couple.

Another search vehicle will leave the Warburton Ranges and travel south along the defence track. The missing pair are believed to have good supplies of food and water.

The area is marked by many small tracks used

[Professor Waring of the WA University to Zoology Department, said today: "They are visiting American zoo-

Searchers find message

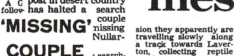

A SIMPLE message in a bottle on a post in desert country has halted a search couple missing Nullar-

sion they apparently are travelling slowly along a track towards Laverton, collecting reptile specimens.

Junction in the desert today.

It found the message in a bottle used as a de-

American Pair Safe

Two Americans, who were believed to be missing in desolate country north of Rawlinna on the trans-Australia railway, arrived in Kalgoorlie on Saturday night unaware that a search party had been looking for them.

They are Dr E. Pianka and his wife Helen, who reported to the Kalgoorlie police after having been told they were thought to be missing.

'MISSING' COUPLE UNAWARE OF ANY SEARCH

Couple On Track Were Not Lost

Two Americans, Dr Eric Pianka and his wife Helen, who had been thought lost north of Rawlinna on the track leading to the Warburton Ranges, have arrived in Perth.

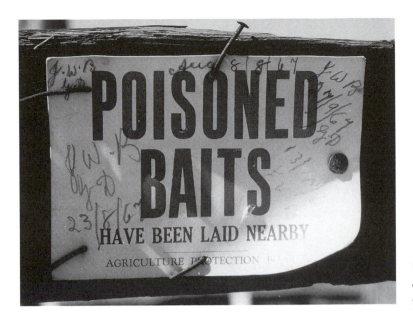

One of dogger Brown's warning signs

Australians take their outback pretty seriously, and rightly so. Nevertheless, it was a real pity that the poor misguided "searchers" had wasted their own valuable time and precious fuel looking for us on a false alarm. That was the first and last time that I ever asked a local for directions. We were both flattered that our ages were underestimated by several years. I certainly did not appreciate being played up as some sort of weirdo "snake cultist." On my last two trips down under, I kept in daily (weekdays) radio contact with the Conservation and Land Management (C.A.L.M.) office in Kalgoorlie.

Some months later, at the same site deep in the desert, I really did manage to get somewhat disoriented while on foot collecting lizards. After tracking down a pair of *Varanus tristis* in a dead marble gum tree, quite a long way away from camp, I had to return to the vehicle for a bow saw to cut open the tree and capture the lizards. I decided not to follow my own circuitous trail back the second time, but endeavored to take a short cut. However, by this time of day the sun was high, and my sense of direction muddled. After walking about a kilometer without seeing the car, I decided that I must have missed it and that I'd better head for the track. I walked and walked without finding the road, continually readjusting my direction in such a way that I thought it would assure that I'd be walking at right angles to the road. The high midday sun made it difficult to gain a good sense of direction. After I'd walked several kilometers without encountering the road, I began to become really concerned. It was getting hot, and I was quite thirsty. I had visions of someone in the future finding my bones out there. When, at last, I finally saw the track off to my right, I was walking almost parallel to it! It took me a good while to walk the four or five kilometers back up the track to camp.

Over the course of sixteen months, we never encountered anyone else out there, though occasionally we did find fresh tire tracks, probably dogger Brown's, as there were strychnine baits and newly erected "Poison Bait" signs in the vicinity. We found *Varanus* that had perished from eating these poisoned baits. We also discovered a flock of very rare parrots, the Princess Parrot, out there.

NOTE TO CHAPTER 6

1. These frogs seem incongruous and totally out of place in the desert. Most of the time, they are inactive, buried deep beneath the surface, encased in a cocoonlike membranous sac, impervious to water loss. When a rare desert rain does fall, they emerge, feed, and breed in ephemeral pools.

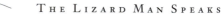

BUSH FLIES

⋅ ⟋⟍⟋⟍ ⋅ ⋅ ⋅ ⋅

MOST WILDERNESS AREAS SUPPORT POPULATIONS OF PESKY arthropods such as ants, gnats, mosquitos, black flies, sand flies, chiggers, ticks, etc., which can make a camping trip quite a miserable experience. There are mossies (mosquitos) in inland Australia at times, and plenty of ants, but the real scourge of the outback is a small relative of the well-known house fly, known locally as the Australian bush fly. Its scientific name is *Musca vetustissima*, the latter species name meaning "silvered with frost." These very abundant small flies, about one-quarter to one-half the size of a housefly, don't actually bite but nevertheless constantly besiege everyone in the outback, swarming around you, landing on your face, and going into eyes, nostrils, mouth, and ears. They seem to be after moisture, and go into a sort of drunken stupor on sweat.

In the winter, there are few bush flies. But at other times of year, particularly during warm summer weather, they reach pestilence levels. One bloke told me of once being able to see a black cloud of flies about two meters thick. At such times, life becomes a horror movie as literally hundreds or even thousands of these face flies descend on you in a virtual cloud of buzzing frantic little insects. You have to experience bush flies to appreciate fully how very trying they can be.

Individual flies make a fair spectrum of sounds: some fly almost silently with only a faint hum, others with a *bzz, brz, brmm,* or even a *vroom.* Each fly has its own individual style, ranging from insulting flybys to more serious inquiries in which a fly might just touch your face briefly and then fly away again, or hover right in front of your nose, or come straight on in to land on your eyeglasses, the tip of your nose, your lips, or cheek, whereupon they generally walk a beeline to your eyes. Some fly very "low," hovering within a millimeter or two of your skin, frequently landing. Often they fly in pairs, tumbling around one another in a sort of dogfight in the air as they careen madly about your head. They remind me of an endless variety of tiny airplanes, ranging from helicopter-like hovercraft to acrobatic biplanes to phantom jets. Some are real kamikazes, coming right in and crawling directly for the nearest orifice (eyes and anuses are preferred). They become frantic and very "sticky" at sunset, as if this is their last chance to drink. Blissfully, when it finally gets dark, they cease activity, and at last you get some respite from the constant droning nuisance (however, on bright moonlit nights, a few flies sometimes still buzz around you). Bush flies cannot fly at all well when it is very cold or very damp, but they still try, looping feebly around.

Bush flies lay their eggs on dung, where the maggot larvae feed and grow before metamorphosing into adult flies. They seem to have few natural enemies, and they occur virtually everywhere throughout interior Australia, even far from areas with livestock. Perhaps they are carried out into the deserts by strong winds. Walking around on carrion and dung as they do, bush flies carry noxious bacteria on their legs, which they deposit on your face, and if possible, in your eyes. Several eye diseases, including the one known as "sandy blight," are transmitted by bush flies.

One quickly learns not to breathe through one's mouth, because inhaling and coughing up a fly is rather an unpleasant experience. Indeed, I once detested my own nostril hairs but have now come to see them from the positive perspective of natural selection as an adaptation to allow respiration in fly-ridden Australia! Eyelashes, ear hair, and ear wax presumably serve a similar function, keeping insects out of your sense organs (a friend of mine once had a beetle crawl into his ear canal!).

Many people wave one hand back and forth in front of their face in an effort to keep the bush flies from settling. This handwaving activity, diagnostic of Australia, has become known as the "Aussie salute." It works, to some extent, as long as the flies are not too sticky. Your cloud of bush flies settles down on your back instead of your face. However, once a fly has landed and actually tasted sweat, it will

Bush flies on Helen's back

not depart even if a hand is waved nearby; such flies must actually be wiped off physically (whereupon they immediately return). After a while, even the most placid people begin to be annoyed by the continuing attendance of all these nasty little pests! Sometimes they are so thick as to overwhelm you. No amount of handwaving will keep them off your face. Eventually a sense of desperation takes over, and you become ready to do almost anything to escape from the flies.

Old-timers wore hats with dozens of corks dangling from the brim on short strings (we tried this, but it didn't work well because the

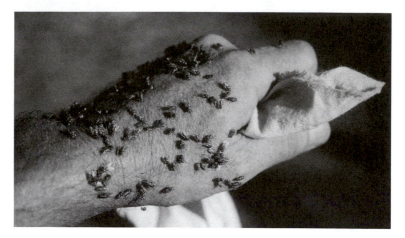

Pesky little buggers!

corks kept getting entangled with one another's leads). We also wore shawls of mosquito netting over our heads, made mesh beekeeper-style hats, and tucked the bottom of the mesh inside our shirt collars. Collars rub, and it is hot inside these, plus they have their own problems, such as interfering with vision, taking a drink, spitting, blowing your nose, etc. Also, you are still plagued by the droning noise and the ever-present flies on your screen mesh right in front of your face, anyway. I have seen pictures of sad bush-fly-beleaguered people sitting around in camp with nylon stockings pulled down over their heads. I have also seen photographs of people perched on tree branches ten feet off ground, trying to eat their dinner in peace (under the questionable assumption that bush flies tend to stay lower down than this). It is lousy finding the dirty little insects in your food. If you are fortunate enough to have a fly-proof haven such as a screened tent or a caravan, you become a prisoner in that flyscreen jail.

Once, I encountered a flyswatter shortage! There wasn't a "flyswat" for sale in all Kalgoorlie. Now I always take a flyswatter from the U.S. down under with me. Most are designed for house flies—sometimes it's hard to find one with holes small enough that bush flies don't go right through them! I fit the rear windows of vehicles with screens to keep the flies out. Upon finishing a lizard trek, we wave our arms about wildly, make a mad dash to the car or van, jump in quickly, grab the flyswatter (which always "lives" on the dashboard), and frantically swat all the flies that came in with us. Indeed, it is an obligation to eradicate your own flies (and, frankly, rather enjoyable after all the suffering they have imposed upon you).

After a while, we discovered a "personal insect repellant" aptly named Scram. Although this did not keep the bush flies from circling and landing, if replenished every half hour or so, it did prevent them from settling down. A daub of Scram on your nose and cheeks meant that if a fly landed there, you could be fairly confident that it would quickly depart! Trust your Scram. We became enamored of, and dependent on, this product and teased about someday doing a Scram commercial: Against a background of the Land Rover way out in the desert, I'd be standing with my foot on a case of Scram, saying that "I'd sooner be out here without water than without Scram." Of course, this stuff will probably prove to be carcinogenic, but without it, we could not have endured the nuisance of bush flies long enough to successfully complete the research.

When bush flies are really thick, performing that basic bodily function which must be fulfilled on a daily basis is rendered quite unpleasant. The flies are much too eager to get at the stuff, to say the least. But you can shed virtually your entire cloud of flies at one fell swoop when you do relieve yourself. Simply dig a steep-sided hole, and after depositing your load in it, wait until the flies have settled down on your fecal material. Then, quickly heave a heaping shovelful of sand on top, and bury them all alive with their favorite stuff. This prevents them from depositing your own feces on your face, too. Of course, you will quickly pick up a new flock of admirers to replenish the ones you just gave the slip, but at least they probably haven't been on human feces. (I don't think that eggs from flies you bury with your turds can successfully grow into maggots underground. I certainly hope they can't!) In some parts of Australia, African dung beetles have been introduced in an effort to reduce the food supply for bush flies (this seems to be working in some areas, but no arid-adapted dung beetles seem to have been released yet).

From time to time, nearly everyone goes mad when confronted with hordes of bush flies. Even a normally placid assistant occasionally comes running into camp wildly waving his/her arms, making a mad dash for the comfort of a screened-in enclosure. I have certainly been driven temporarily insane by bush flies, as the next two paragraphs will show. I've had a lot of time to meditate about the pleasure I feel when I squash a particularly pesky face fly! In an effort to retain my sanity, I play a little game I call "Out of my face" or "Save Face," which may actually be a descent into insanity. This is rather like a real-life version of some computer shooting games such as "Apple

Invaders" or "Space Eggs," except that it is better than a computer game in that it is more complex: three-dimensional, not so precisely repetitious, and can be played against a myriad of ever-changing natural backgrounds.

Think of your face as fly bait and the zone immediately in front and around it as a three-dimensional war zone. Flies are the enemy "targets" which come on endlessly, and in an infinite variety. If you miss one, it will return, and give you as many chances at it as you need. There is always another in a never-ending continuous supply, and the "game" never ends (it is also free). The object is to down as many enemy aircraft as possible. It is imperative to keep one arm free for flies at all times—I reserve my left arm as a flyswatter. Holding my left hand slightly cupped, with thumb and fingers pressed tightly together just in front of my specs at the left side of my face, I plunge ahead into the fly field.

Some skill is required to know just when to swat ("shoot"), but after a bit of practice you can down most of the flies that insist upon frequenting that small and very personal zone immediately in front of your face, smashing them against your right shoulder. Bush flies are quite tough and durable, and it is a good idea to grind your palm into your shoulder with a side-to-side twist before raising your hand (otherwise, lots of "hits" escape!). Then, with a disdainful flick, you can send their mangled little corpses spinning down to the hot sand. I like to think of the red, white, and black splotches of fly blood, guts, and eggs on my right shoulder as badges for shooting prowess. (I am an "ace," having gotten as many as a dozen flies with a single swat!) If you wear eyeglasses, you must take care not to hit your specs or you will injure your own nose (and perhaps break your glasses). Another problem with this game is the stench of feces and dead animals that accumulates on your left palm and right shoulder! This has its own limited advantages in that more flies are attracted to the smell, making them vulnerable to being squashed. You can always wash your hands and change your shirt. I am convinced that there are real payoffs to this game, too—not only do you relieve your own hostilities, but you also reduce the number of flies, and select against those that insist on being in your face. Indeed, if everyone would play "Out of my face," Australian bush flies would be both fewer and better behaved.

BUSH FIRES

· · · · · · · · ·

LIGHTNING REGULARLY SETS HUNDREDS OF FIRES ANNUALLY in Australia, especially during November through January. In a study of over 5,000 fires in spinifex country of the Northern Territory over the thirty-five-year period from 1950 through 1984, there were an average of 143 natural wildfires per year, most caused by lightning (Griffin et al. 1983). During that same period of time, there was a movement of Aborigines out of the bush, reducing the numbers of fires started by humans. There has recently been an increasing movement of Aborigines back to reside on tribal lands, except that nowadays Aborigines seldom walk, preferring to ride in vehicles. They still set fires, but seldom very far from tracks. Some of these fires are capricious. When a car carrying Aborigines broke down in October of 1989 along a little used track, the stranded Aborigines lit the spinifex to send a smoke signal to their peers to the north. Strong winds quickly whipped this fire into a frenzy, and it broke up into several fires, one of which I watched as it burned for the next month in a great loop traveling many dozens of kilometers.

A comparison of the frequency and extent of wildfires in the chaparral vegetation of southern California with those of similar areas in adjacent Baja California is most informative (Minnich 1983). Although fire prevention and fire-fighting activities on the populated U.S. side of the border reduced the frequency of small fires, in this fire-protected region the largest fires were much more extensive than they were across the border in sparsely developed Mexico, where frequent small burns act as fire breaks and prevent extensive burns from taking place. Large fires homogenize the landscape, reducing habitat heterogeneity.

Spinifex tussocks are perfectly designed for combustion, consisting of hemispherical clumps of numerous matchstick-sized blades of dry curled grass filled with flammable resins, loosely interpenetrating one another, and laced with ample air spaces. With such ideal tinder, one match is all it takes to start a fire. Spinifex has been called an "ideal pyrophyte" (Pyne 1991). Bush fires are regularly started naturally by lightning, raging completely out of control for weeks across many square kilometers of desert. Thunderstorms and lightning are frequent during summer. Lightning-induced wildfires are most prevalent during November and December. Long after sunset, one sees the eerie red glow of a wildfire on some horizon other than the western one. On several occasions when a wildfire was burning nearby, I have lain awake nights concerned about escaping from a wall of flames. Most marble gum trees have charred dark hollows, and charcoal from old burns litters the ground everywhere in the Great Victoria Desert. *Eucalyptus* trees are fire-resistant, and frequently survive a burn. Both spinifex and mallee rejuvenate themselves rapidly, from live roots as well as by seedling establishment.

Fires were once a major agent of disturbance in all grassland and semidesert biomes, including African savannas and the North American tallgrass prairies. Most of these ecosystems have now been reduced to mere vestiges, and controlled burning or fire control is practiced by humans virtually everywhere. The inland Australian desert is one of the last existing areas where natural wildfires still remain a regular and dominant feature of an extensive natural landscape largely undisturbed by humans. In this region, an important fire succession cycle generates spatial and temporal heterogeneity in microhabitats and habitats. By maintaining a mosaic of habitats, these regional processes facilitate local diversity.

The very flammable hummock grass plant life form is unique to Australia. Deserts in other regions, such as the Sonoran desert of North America, do not usually accumulate enough combustible material to carry fires. Fires do occur regularly in the Kalahari semidesert of southern Africa, an open savanna woodland, but do not seem to reticulate to as great an extent as fires do in Australia. Fires are a predictable event in arid Australia, particularly in spinifex grasslands. All spinifex communities are in a state of cyclic develop-

Spinifex is almost perfect tinder.

ment from fire to fire. In 1967 in the Northern Territory, only about 20 percent of some 150,000 square kilometers of spinifex habitat was in a "mature" climax state, with the other 80 percent either in regenerative stages following fires or in a degenerative state owing to drought (Allan and Griffin 1986; Griffin et al. 1983). A single fire in this region during the 1960s covered about 10,000 square kilometers or about 7 percent of the total area of spinifex habitat. An even larger fire in 1982–1983 burned 30,000 square kilometers (about 20 percent of the spinifex habitat). As indicated above, hundreds of fires, most set by lightning, occur here each year.

With such exceedingly high levels of disturbance, a fairly rapid rate of recovery is to be expected. Fire return intervals are short; within four to five years many areas will carry another burn. Burned plots converge on their original state quickly; in seven years, dry weight production of spinifex can total over 800 kilograms per hectare, approximately one quarter of the standing crop of "mature" stands at nearby sites (Winkworth 1967). Time required for a burned stand to reach maturity is a function of precipitation, and it may take as long as twenty to twenty-five years, sometimes even longer. The probability of a burn increases with time, and cumulative precipitation, since the last burn.

A study area consisting of a meadow of long-unburned mature spinifex in seed

The combined effects of these forces on animals and their micro-habitats are drastic and exceedingly heterogeneous in space. Certain lizard species are arboreal and associated with fire-resistant trees. These are relatively unaffected by fire. Many or even most individual lizards sometimes survive such burns, although survivorship is doubt-lessly reduced for some time afterward. Fires attract hawks and crows, which feed on fire-killed animals and take advantage of the lack of cover to catch survivors. By virtue of their ectothermy, many lizards may be able to become inactive and remain underground for a month or more until the vegetation and insect fauna above recover.

Population densities of certain lizard species, such as *Ctenophorus fordi* and *Ctenophorus isolepis,* are actually greater on recently burned areas. Many other desert lizard species, including *Ctenophorus inermis* and *Ctenotus calurus*, with open habitat requirements, presumably reinvade or repopulate burned areas rapidly, quickly reaching high densities in their "preferred" open habitat (such species usually persist at very low densities even in mature stands of dense, closed-in spinifex). Other lizard species, such as *Delma butleri, Cyclodomorphus melanops*, and *Diplodactylus elderi,* require large spinifex tussocks for microhabitats and presumably nearly vanish over extensive open areas following a burn. However, such "climax" species continue to exist as relics in the isolated pockets and patches of habitat that escaped burning. If a species does go extinct in one patch of habitat, it can reinvade from another patch at a later time. Animals with active habitat selection (such as Australian desert lizards) can reach ecological and evolutionary stable equilibria between "source" habitats and "sink" habitats, with dispersal from the former to the latter maintaining species locally (Pulliam 1988).

Following a fire caused by lightning, sands are frequently wetted by thundershowers, facilitating rapid growth of spinifex from both live roots as well as by seedling establishment. Newly burned areas are quite open, with lots of bare ground and tiny, well-spaced clumps of *Triodia*. Unburned patches, in contrast, are composed of large ancient tussocks, frequently quite close together with little open space between them. As time progresses, *Triodia* clumps grow, which simultaneously increases the amount of combustible material and reduces the gaps between tussocks, thereby increasing the probability that another fire will be carried.

Throughout this process, lizard microhabitats (cover) and associated food resources change gradually. In both birds and lizards, species present on recently burned areas represent a subset of those present on more mature climax sites. Relative abundances of species also fluctuate substantially through succession, with some common species becoming quite rare. Rare species do not always remain rare and may be vitally important to hold an ecosystem together, allowing the system to respond to changing environmental conditions. The prey spectrum for a recently burned area differs from that of less recently burned areas; the former has relatively fewer termites but more spiders (Pianka 1989). Presumably, by destroying litter and spinifex, fires reduce cellulose availability, hence reducing food supplies for termites. Fairly mature unburned sites in the Great Victoria Desert have a very high abundance of termites.

About a dozen species of mid-sized marsupial mammals, including hare wallabies, have gone extinct in the Australian interior during the past half century. Andrew Burbidge and colleagues (1988) discovered this only recently by taking museum skins out into the desert and interviewing older Aborigines about their youth. Approximate dating was accomplished by recalling airplane traffic over Australia during the Second World War. Aborigines not only remembered many species now extinct as being abundant during the 1940s, but also provided many localities. Theories as to the cause of the disappearance of mid-sized marsupials include competition with introduced rabbits and camels, as well as predation by introduced feral cats and foxes. The removal of Aboriginal human populations, and their effect via increased incidence of burning, could also be a factor. Australian authorities are now attempting to increase burning and to mimic Aboriginal burning patterns to create a spatial mosaic of fire-disturbed habitat patches of differing ages and sizes, and to prevent the homogenization of the landscape that occurs as a result of extensive large fires. Also, attempts are now being made to remove foxes locally and to re-introduce some species of mid-sized marsupials from stocks taken from offshore islands where populations have been able to persist in the absence of fox predation.

Satellite imagery offers earth scientists a powerful tool for studying a wide variety of large-scale phenomena, ranging from geology to oceanography to meteorology. Unfortunately, this potent new methodology comes a bit too late for large-scale biology, since extensive areas remaining undisturbed by human activities are few. Inland desert areas of Australia constitute an important exception: here cloud cover is low or nonexistent most of the time, and excellent imagery is the rule, greatly facilitating analyses. Whereas ash absorbs infrared radiation, unburned vegetation reflects it. Even after rains or wind wash or blow away ash, reflectance properties of burned versus unburned areas differ markedly, allowing sharp delineation of fire boundaries. The sizes and geometry of fires are readily measured, and fire scars can be traced through time (Pianka 1992).

In such a large natural region, habitat patches at different stages of post-fire recovery can reach dynamic equilibrium, with new burns continually arising via the "death" of more combustible, and more vulnerable, older stages of succession (a quasi-stationary distribution is reached). A two-dimensional frequency distribution of the ages and sizes of fire scars can be estimated and examined to see if it constitutes a stationary distribution. Reflectance properties recorded from space could allow inference of the present state of biotas on the ground, as well as the climate during the immediate past. The extent to which temporal changes in multispectral reflectance patterns at a given site can be extrapolated to geographic patterns in space needs to be ascertained by careful fieldwork. Although a great deal more remains to be known, monitoring habitats and biotic diversity from satellites could ultimately prove to be possible, at least in arid regions.

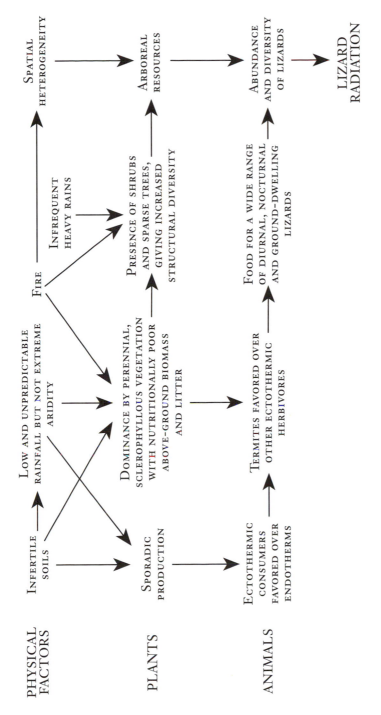

SPATIAL HETEROGENEITY → ARBOREAL RESOURCES → ABUNDANCE AND DIVERSITY OF LIZARDS → LIZARD RADIATION

INFREQUENT HEAVY RAINS → PRESENCE OF SHRUBS AND SPARSE TREES, GIVING INCREASED STRUCTURAL DIVERSITY

FIRE

LOW AND UNPREDICTABLE RAINFALL BUT NOT EXTREME ARIDITY → DOMINANCE BY PERENNIAL, SCLEROPHYLLOUS VEGETATION WITH NUTRITIONALLY POOR ABOVE-GROUND BIOMASS AND LITTER → TERMITES FAVORED OVER OTHER ECTOTHERMIC HERBIVORES → FOOD FOR A WIDE RANGE OF DIURNAL, NOCTURNAL AND GROUND-DWELLING LIZARDS

INFERTILE SOILS

SPORADIC PRODUCTION

ECTOTHERMIC CONSUMERS FAVORED OVER ENDOTHERMS

PHYSICAL FACTORS

PLANTS

ANIMALS

FIGURE 8
Morton and James' (1988) megahypothesis explaining the high lizard diversity in arid Australia

At least a dozen different factors contribute to the exceedingly high diversity of lizards in arid Australia. These include (1) unpredictable rainfall, (2) nutrient-poor soils, (3) the unique hummock life form and physical structure of *Triodia* grasses, (4) the low nutrient content of spinifex, (5) abundant and diverse termite faunas, (6) nocturnality, (7) fossoriality (sand swimming), (8) arboreality, (9) habitat specificity, (10) usurpation of ecological roles occupied by other taxa elsewhere, (11) biogeographic and historical factors, and (12) a complex fire succession cycle that creates and maintains habitat variety via disturbance, as described above. Most of these mechanisms were put together into a megahypothesis by Morton and James (1988; see also Pianka 1989). Figure 8 summarizes their proposed causal network with some of my own additions. Unpredictable precipitation, nutrient-poor soils, and wildfires are the driving physical variables. Primary productivity is scant and erratic, favoring spinifex grasses that are poor in nitrogen, and thus relatively unusable fodder for most herbivores except termites, which in turn constitute a food resource that is particularly suitable for ectothermic lizards. Moreover, periodic heavy rainfall promotes woody vegetation (*Acacia* shrubs, mulga, and marble gum trees), thereby supporting arboreal and litter-dwelling species of lizards. Although fire and fire-induced spatial heterogeneity were not included in Morton and James' scheme, they are easily added (Pianka 1992).

AUSTRALIAN
ABORIGINES

FEW PEOPLE CAN CLAIM TO BE EXPERTS ON A SUBJECT AS vast and complex as the diverse tribes of Australian Aborigines. I have only met and spoken with a handful of these people and would never claim to be an expert. However, I have observed some of them at a distance over the past quarter of a century and have also done some anthropological reading. Discussions with a wide variety of knowledgeable people have been quite informative, too.

In the United States, minority groups, such as Americans of African and Mexican descent, are extremely sensitive as to what they are called. Early on, the former preferred to be called "Negroes," then "Blacks," but now "African Americans." The sequence for those of Mexican descent has been "Mexican Americans," "Chicanos," "Hispanics," and lately for increased political clout, "Latinos." Something similar has happened in Australia, with the native Australians now being referred to as "Aboriginals" rather than the earlier "Abos" or "Aborigines." One day they may graduate to "Native Australians."

As noted earlier, in terms of geological time, the arrival of native Aboriginal humans in Australia is a relatively recent event, now thought to have occurred about 50,000 years ago, although some authorities think that it could have been as long ago as 120,000 years. At that time, sea levels were considerably lower than they are today— New Guinea, mainland Australia, and Tasmania were joined as a supercontinent (Aborigines presumably walked across the Torres and Bass straits on land bridges). Australian Aborigines have been on the island continent for less than 0.01 percent of its long geological history (even so, that is five hundred times longer than Europeans and Asians have been in Australia). Much more recently, probably within the past 5,000 to 8,000 years, Aborigines brought in the dingo, the first carnivorous placental mammal, which probably caused the extinction of the largest predatory marsupial on mainland Australia, the thylacine. Where Australian Aborigines came from is even more uncertain than when they arrived (there may well have been several immigrations). Rising sea levels have inundated coastal campsites where early humans first camped, and destroyed fossil evidence.

In his journal, Captain Cook had the following to say about the Aborigines:

"The natives do not appear to be numberous neither do they seem to live in large bodies but dispers'd in small parties along the water side; those I saw were about as tall as Europeans, of a very dark brown color but not black nor had they wooly frizled hair, but black, and lank much like ours. No sort of cloathing or ornaments were ever seen by any one of us upon any one of them or in or about any of their hutts, from which I conclude that they never wear any . . . However we could not know but very little of their customs as we never were able to form any connections with them, they had not so much as touch'd the things we had left in their hutts on purpose for them to take away . . . From what I have said of the Natives of New Holland they may appear to some to be the most wretched people upon Earth, but in reality they are far more happier than we Europeans; being wholly unacquainted not only with the superfluous but the necessary Conveniences so much sought after in Europe, they are happy in not knowing the use of them. They live in a Tranquillity which is not disturb'd by the Inequality of Condition: the Earth and sea of their own accord furnishes them with all things necessary for life, they covet not Magnificent Houses, Household-stuff &c., they live in a warm and fine Climate and enjoy a very wholsome air, so that they have very little need of Clothing and this they seem to be fully sencible of, for many to whome we gave Cloth &c. to, left it carelessly upon the Sea beach and in the woods as a thing they had no manner of use for. In short they seem'd to set no Value upon any thing of their own for any one article we could offer them; this in my own opinion argues that they think themselves provided with all the necessarys of Life and that they have no superfluities." (BAGLIN AND MULLINS 1969)

Iron and glass, however, were soon prized by Aborigines for their hardness and were used to make tools and weapons, some of which were traded over long distances from tribe to tribe. Such "trade routes" are also evidenced by seashells in the interior and by central Australian boomerangs on the north coast. A knife or a hatchet was a prized possession, used until it broke or wore down to nothing.

Most early explorers and historians of Australia commented on the extent to which the Aborigines exploited fire. Spinifex grasses give off dark smoke, which can be seen from afar. Australian Aborigines used fire to send long-distance smoke signals, to manage habitats, and to keep terrain open, as well as to facilitate capture of various animals for food. Some think that the extensive grasslands in Australia were formed and maintained by regular Aboriginal burning, and that Aborigines acted to select members of plant communities for resistance to fire or for an ability to come back quickly following a fire.

Whereas most tribal groups must have hugged the coast, a few penetrated the inland desert. Like the San Bushmen of the Kalahari, these desert people developed almost uncanny and enviable survival skills in the arid inland. They not only learned how to find water in an almost waterless terrain, but they also figured out which plants were edible (including some toxic ones that could be detoxified) and how to capture most kinds of animals. Valuable tricks were discovered that aided in capturing various animals—a fleeing goanna could often be stopped dead in its tracks by issuing an imitation of the call of a certain hawk, which made the lizard a much easier target for a throwing stick. Aborigines can throw a small stick (or a spear) with great accuracy, hitting the extremely delicate head of a goanna from a substantial distance. One of these big lizards is viewed as "bush tucker," a sort of a free hamburger.

Twenty-five years ago, I encountered four Aboriginal men—with a young camel hitched to a rickety cast-off old trailer with a bent axle—gathering sandalwood in the desert east of Laverton. They had a flat tire, but no tools with which to repair it. After helping them stuff the tire with spinifex and get it back on the rim with my tire-repair tools, I headed out into the desert with my own complex life-support system (a four-wheel-drive Land Rover, fifty gallons of gasoline, and fifty gallons of water, plus a two-way RFDS radio), marveling the whole way that they were carrying neither food nor water, let alone spare parts or a radio, just "firewood."

Desert dwellers were highly nomadic, carrying their scant posses-

sions with them. They went naked, except for a rope around their waist used for carrying things such as lizard prey. To sleep naked on a cold, clear desert night under the stars is no small achievement. As every camper knows, you can be cozily warm on the side facing a campfire, but freezing on the other (standing people usually rotate their backs to the fire, then their fronts). For warmth when they sleep, Aborigines cleverly build two fires, one on either side; as the fires die down, Aborigines roll toward one of the two fires. Toward dawn, many finish up by rolling right onto the hot coals (many Aborigines used to sport fire scars). That's one way to wake up quickly! On a cold night, Aborigines like to sleep huddled with their dingoes. Indeed, on their quaint temperature scale, a "five-dog night" is a pretty chilly one. Accounts of waking Aborigines following a long, bitterly cold night are interesting—apparently, to keep the core temperature of their torsos and heads at viable levels, the circulation to their arms and legs is cut off, and, as these appendages get very cold, they become numb and "go to sleep." To help get the blood flowing again in the morning, an Aborigine must flail his or her arms and legs about, banging them against the ground. These are pretty tough people.

Aborigines have an exceedingly rich and interesting mythology of so-called dreamtime stories about the origins of the sun and moon, the creation of various topographic features, weather, the ecological role of humans, as well as innumerable very interesting myths about other species, including some that have now gone extinct (some think that Aboriginal hunting pressures may have caused the extinction of the Pleistocene megafauna). Aborigines believe that the dead go on living as spirits which must be appeased so that they don't pester or kill the living. Spirits range from the tiny, harmless leprechaun-like mimi, which are as thin as a sheet of paper and hide in tight crevices, to a variety of terrible mamandi, many of which eat people. A favored persistent watering hole is said to be blessed with a friendly spirit, and if that spirit is offended and driven away, the water hole will dry up.

Another large, dangerous spirit is the bunyip. The rainbow serpent can be either benevolent or dangerous, assuming many different forms. As a gigantic snake, the rainbow serpent formed meandering river courses as it crawled over the surface in the "dreamtime" (when the sun and the stars and earth and all its features were formed). One provocative legend links the tides with the moon, asserting that high tides fill the moon so that it balloons out and becomes full, whereas at neap tides all the water flows out of the moon until it becomes just a thin sliver. The Sun woman and the Moon man are the spirits of Aborigines who refused to die. The Milky Way is a celestial stream full of cosmic fish. There are legends for each of the planets as well as for most of the prominent stars, with each representing some long-deceased, but still-remembered and named, ancestor. Certain of these spirits are thought to protect particular species (usually their own favored food) from overexploitation by Aborigines.

Consider a more detailed example of one such Aboriginal legend, which tells about how two species of monitor lizards (*Varanus tristis*, and *V. giganteus*, the perentie) got their coloring by painting each other. The perentie went first and did a beautiful artistic job painting scales in a sort of rosette pattern on the smaller *tristis* (an accurate description of the coloration of *tristis*). But when the *tristis*'s turn came, about halfway through it grew tired of painting the big perentie, and finished up by just throwing its bucket of paint on the back half of the perentie (perenties are colored more or less in such a pattern). The legend finishes with the statement that to this day, perenties keep *tristis* in the trees on account of their ancient betrayal (also an accurate statement about the habits of these lizards).

Australian Aborigines are extremely artistic, using red and yellow ochres, white clay, and black charcoal mixed with fat for paints. Elaborate rock paintings can be found across the continent. Bark paintings of northern tribes depict legends, often showing "X-ray" versions of both animals and humans, accurately depicting bones, muscles, and internal organs. I acquired three such bark paintings in Darwin, painted by Lipundja at the Milingimbi Mission in Arnhem Land. The largest one measures a full 24" by 42", and depicts a scene at a water hole with an anhinga (a predatory aquatic bird, also known as a "diver" or a darter), a water monitor lizard, a snake, plus many fish and yams. The following description is pasted on the back side:

Djambarrpuynu Mortality Rites

The above cycle tells in song and dance the habits of the various flora and fauna found in and around a certain water hole on the nearby mainland. Here a large freshwater goanna is attacking a grass snake, whilst nearby a diver prepares to plunge upon unsuspecting fish. Around the water hole grow many yams.

This large aquatic monitor lizard, *Varanus mertensi*, was not described scientifically until 1951! Recently, a new style based on sand painting in central Australia has emerged: painted now on canvas, thousands of colorful dots depict important scenes from various dreamtime myths.

Aborigines have a complex kinship system, which not only prohibits inbreeding but also assures that everyone has relatives no matter what happens to his/her own direct kin. The social life of Aborigines is elaborate. A tribal gathering, termed a "Corroboree," with dancing and singing, often lasts all night. They are also musically inclined, making haunting melodies on the didgeridoo (a large hollowed wooden horn). Perhaps the most interesting of all among these many ceremonies are the initiation rites—when a boy becomes a man (and is thereafter allowed to take a woman as a mate). Boys are held down by men and circumcised. In some tribes, to ascend to the next higher level in the hierarchy, a male is subincised (the bottom side of his penis is opened up). It is intriguing to speculate that this could constitute a cultural form of birth control!

Aboriginal societies are traditionally strongly sexist, with activities and important rites that are the exclusive domain of members of one

sex. Initiation ceremonies are "men's business." Ceremonial rights are also hierarchical, with the oldest, wisest people most privy to all. At certain ceremonies restricted to initiated males only, a flattened stick known to whites as a "bull roarer" is twirled around, making a loud buzzing noise. This is a signal for all females and uninitiated males to stay well away. The penalty for seeing something to which one is not entitled is often death. There is a sharp division of labor between men and women. Men range more widely and hunt larger quarry such as kangaroos, whereas women forage somewhat closer to camp, gathering edible plants and smaller animals such as lizards. Often, the women begin to deplete their resources before the men and urge moving on to a new campsite before the present area becomes overexploited.

Tribal customs are referred to collectively by traditional Aborigines these days as "the law." They have their own special recipes for cooking each of their foods. For example, there is only one proper way to prepare and cook a goanna. Using a hooked stick, the goanna's stomach and intestines are first extracted out of its mouth and discarded (it would not do to cut the animal open!). The intact animal is then flamed over a fire and buried under hot sand and ashes for about ten to fifteen minutes until it begins to sizzle, when it is removed. The skin peels away easily, exposing the succulent, juicy white meat (fat bodies and the tail are preferred). When Aborigines are hungry, they eat the entire lizard except for its head (even the brains are often sucked out). In times of severe food scarcity, after the soft parts are picked off, the bony remains are crushed with rocks, and even these are consumed.

As indicated earlier, bush flies lay their eggs on dung and carry noxious bacteria around on their legs, which they deposit on your face and, if possible, in your eyes. Bush flies transmit several nasty eye diseases, including one known as "sandy blight." Australian Aborigines sometimes go blind due to eye infections developed as a result of bush flies. Some are said to allow a bush fly to walk across their eyes without even blinking! I have a feeling for what this must be like, as bush flies often walk eerily across the lens of my eyeglasses. It is terrible when a bush fly gets beneath your glasses—you must drop everything and use your finger to wipe the damn bug out!

Aborigines are expert trackers. Their children are said to amuse themselves by tracking ants. Though this may sound preposterous, it might actually be possible in low light in very soft dust. Sands leave

a record of what creatures have moved past. Winds regularly dull and erase all tracks. On overcast days or during midday when the sun is high, tracks are difficult to see. The best times for tracking are when the sun is low in the sky and shadows are long, during morning and afternoon. Tracks are best seen by looking into the light. With experience, you soon learn to judge the "run" of the track, that is, where the animal is headed, almost becoming the animal yourself. This allows one to move ahead quickly, cutting the track at intervals, to find the animal rapidly. The approximate age of a track can be determined by its crispness, and by whether or not other tracks, such as those of nocturnal species, cross over the track in question. A crisp new track less than an hour old will lead you to the maker of that track. It is a line guaranteed to lead you to food!

As indicated earlier, a great deal can be learned about wary, unobservable species such as *Varanus* by tracking these large lizards across sandy areas. Sometimes, the track suddenly becomes the magnificent animal, captured in mid-stride and frozen in time. More

often than not, however, long before you see it, the animal breaks into
a run and dives down a hole or climbs up a tree, escaping into a hollow.
Often, the track of a running animal is harder to follow than that of
one walking. In many ways, what I have been doing as a scientist in

arid Australia is simply rediscovering, and writing down in scientific English, what many Aborigines once knew long ago.

The easy way of life offered by whites lured large numbers of Aborigines to missions, stations, and outlying villages. Some were relocated more or less forcefully. During the late 1960s, a concerted effort was made to make contact with the last wild Aborigines in the Great Sandy Desert. For several decades, from about the 1950s through the early 1980s, few Aborigines lived in the desert, although many often went "walkabout" for short periods of time. The abrupt removal of Aborigines must have reduced the numbers of bush fires, although lightning regularly sets hundreds of fires annually, especially during November through January.

In what has befallen the Australian Aborigines, there are many parallels to what happened to the American Indians. Most white people had little or no use for wild Aborigines: one colonist wrote, "Whenever I encounter men on my land, I shoot them, because they are cattle killers; the women too, because they give birth to cattle killers; the children as well, because they would become cattle killers." Many Aborigines were hunted down like animals and simply shot. Some were deliberately poisoned with strychnine. Their lands were taken from them, leaving them unable to fend for themselves. They were chained and imprisoned for killing sheep and cattle to feed themselves. Smallpox, syphilis, leprosy, influenzas, and Christianity are just some of the European diseases that have ravaged these unfortunate people. Entire tribes have died out. Aborigines were worked hard for next to nothing in pay, fed poorly out by the woodpile, given used tea leaves and shoddy goods. They were not even treated like second-class citizens, but more like dogs or slaves. Their women, called gins and lubras, were regularly molested by white men. Babies of mixed race were taken away from their biological mothers and sent to white foster homes in the cities, to be raised as whites. Relatively few "full-blooded" Aborigines still exist. Incredibly, Aborigines were not given "citizenship" in their own country until 1967. Before then, they had virtually no rights and were supposedly under the "protection" of a corrupt Aboriginal affairs board, which was empowered to run their lives, and which moved Aborigines to "settlements" that were in fact more like prisons. To get an exemption entitling them to the rights of a white person, half-castes or Aborigines had to give up all contacts with their people and "live like a white man."

One tribal group was divided and separated during the Second World War when the British exploded atomic bombs on the surface at Maralinga in South Australia, creating a vast radioactive no-man's-land. Recently, the federal government built several hundred miles of roads in the desert interior expressly for the vehicular movement of Aborigines along some of their ancient "dreaming trails." To ease its guilt further, the Australian government sends each Aborigine a monthly check, many of which are immediately spent on grog. Alcoholism has been exceedingly destructive. Aboriginal culture, and the rich lore of natural history formerly passed on from generation to generation, is rapidly vanishing. Old cars abandoned by Aborigines, as well as beer and wine bottles and other litter, now line outback tracks.

Not surprisingly, after being disenfranchised so completely and for so long, emerging Aboriginal rights groups (usually with a militant white advisor) are seeking power and land tenure. One such group was camped out for a while at the old Swan Brewery in Perth, claiming that it was a sacred site. There is an attitude of racial superiority among many whites and a tendency to dispute Aboriginal claims of sacred sites, especially when these come into conflict with big business interests (usually mining). Groups of Aborigines have now moved back out into the bush and set up "communities." Some community elders have prohibited liquor within their lands in an effort to dry out their people. One community does not allow petrol vehicles on their lands because petrol sniffing irreversibly damaged the minds of many of their members (diesel fumes don't give a "high").

To date, no one has yet undertaken a serious effort to census the lizards at a site in the remote Great Sandy Desert—wanting to undertake this overdue project, I applied to the Department of Conservation and Land Management (C.A.L.M.) for a permit to collect in the Rudall River National Park. They first granted me an unconditional permit, but then quickly sent me an amended permit which required that I obtain the consent of the local Aboriginal group in residence. Unbeknownst to me, this community equates C.A.L.M. with big mining operations, and is asserting its rights to the land at Rudall River. Their disappointing response to my letter asking for permission to study lizards was direct and to the point: "Unfortunately, at this time, [we] are extremely busy until the end of the year.

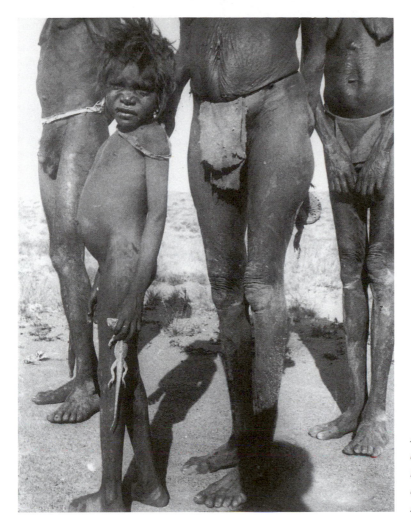

An Aboriginal child holding a lizard like a candy bar—it will soon be eaten.

Could you please postpone your visit to this area for the time being, and write again next year when the Martu should not be so busy." Since this was a once-in-a-lifetime opportunity from my own per-spective, effectively the Great Sandy Desert must remain unstudied (by me, at least).

KALAHARI
AND NAMIB

Ten

In 1969–1970, WITH THE ABLE ASSISTANCE OF MY GOOD
friend and colleague Ray Huey, I was extremely fortunate to be able
to extend my intercontinental comparisons to include a third independently evolved desert-lizard system, the Kalahari semidesert of
southern Africa. In terms of its climate and physiography, the
Kalahari Desert is virtually identical to the Great Victoria Desert in
Australia. Both areas have summer rains and stabilized long red
sandridges running parallel to the strongest prevailing winds. Indeed,
without their characteristic plants and animals, one would be hard
pressed to distinguish between these two regions on the basis of
physical environments alone. Their biotas, however, are very different and distinctive.

In the Kalahari, large placental ungulates abound, including
steenbok, springbok, gemsbok, hartebeest, eland, and wildebeest.
These in turn support many large and small predators, including
lions, leopards, cheetahs, hyaenas, jackals, bat-eared foxes, mon-
gooses, and exquisitely beautiful suricates (called "meercats" by
Afrikaners). Most lizard families (agamids, geckos, skinks, and varanids)
are shared by both deserts, although a few differ (pygopodids in
Australia, chameleons and lacertids in Africa). Species richness of
lizards in the Kalahari is only about half that found in Australia,
however. As to snakes, in addition to the elapids, Africa also has
viperids (true hinged-fang venomous snakes), including the exceed-

ingly formidable puff adder. I have always been fascinated by cobras, and it was a real treat and a great thrill to encounter them in the wild!

Sociable Weavers are small, sparrowlike, ploceid birds that nest communally, with their nest entrances facing downward. A nest looks rather like a large haystack up in a tree (where there are few trees, these birds build nests on the crossbars of telephone and power poles). As their colonies expand, nests sometimes become so heavy that they pull down the tree. I had been told that almost every Sociable Weaver nest colony has a resident cobra living within it. This is an excellent arrangement for the snakes, which eat eggs and baby birds (it is rather like one of us living in a grocery store!).[1] As we drove past one such colony, I thought I saw a snake, so we stopped to take a closer look. Sure enough, there was a rather contorted, kinky, dead-looking snake twisted up in the nest about five meters above ground. We began tossing sticks up at it to see if it was alive, and it began to move! When one of us hit the snake, it raised its head and hooded! We continued to bombard it with sticks until it tried to crawl away, and then it eventually lost its purchase and fell to the ground, where we teased it to make it hood, then photographed it. Some cape cobras are a beautiful golden color.

Even though southern Africa is not usually considered "down under," it is in the Southern Hemisphere and is definitely a part of this story. We set up ten study areas in the Kalahari, including two within the Kalahari Gemsbok National Park, a large nature reserve with herds of half a dozen species of antelope plus the full spectrum of large predators, including both leopard and lion. Tourists are allowed within the park only during daylight hours. One of the advantages of being biologists, however, is that we were able to make a convincing case that we had to camp out within the park in order to collect geckos at night.

Geckoing was a dangerous and fear-filled business with lions and leopards on the prowl. Every individual big cat is known to the park authorities, and it is strictly illegal to shoot one for any reason. Even so, we applied for, and were given, a permit to carry a .45-caliber pistol for use in self-defense (this probably wouldn't stop a lion, but we fully intended to go down fighting if attacked!). We were warned repeatedly never ever to turn our backs on, or to run from, a big cat. With considerable trepidation, we ventured out into the dark African night to look for geckos by eyeshine, staying as close to the vehicle as possible. However, geckoing was extremely ineffective because we couldn't help but scan the black distance in a 360° sweep every few minutes, checking for the big eyeshine of predators (you need to look much closer to spot geckos). A lagomorph known as a springhare was quite common, and these rodents had large bright eyeshine. Whenever we saw one, we had to watch it until it bounced away to reassure ourselves that it was harmless.

Once we finished collecting all the species of geckos we expected on an area inside the park, we ceased geckoing because of the risk. However, at one study site deep within the park, we had not been able to collect one highly expected, but elusive, species of gecko by the end of the study. On our last night out at this study site, we were joined by a South African biologist. At a water hole only about four to five kilometers away from our camp that day, he had seen fresh tracks of a large lone male lion (the most dangerous because without females, males are usually hungry and ill-tempered). So on that last night out we were all quite keyed up, with smokers chain smoking away. At five- to ten-minute intervals, one of us would climb up on top of a vehicle and scan the horizon with a portable spotlight. We tried to stay close to the vehicles and to each other. I was geckoing with Larry Coons, with each of us responsible for our 180° of horizon, walking silently along about ten or fifteen meters apart from one another. Suddenly, Larry whispered, "Eric, right between us!" We had walked right up on a serval, a long-legged cat about the size of a bobcat, without even seeing it! Soon thereafter, we gave up geckoing and had to leave the elusive missing species of gecko as "highly expected."

We often enjoyed one of Ray Huey's delicious hot curries with chutney sauce for dinner. One night, Huey got a craving for a chicken-pea-rice casserole. Trouble was, we didn't have any of the ingredients. Undaunted, Ray substituted a can of beef stew for the chicken, and some Tastix ("looks like rice, tastes like rice, but is cheaper than rice") for the rice—we had nothing that would substitute for peas. Larry and I refused to eat the resulting concoction, but, like any good cook, Ray ate some as a matter of principle. He then made some greasy popcorn, using too much oil. Some component of the stew (probably the meat) must have been off—in any case, poor old Ray passed out on his cot for several hours (he didn't even go geckoing, which meant that he felt really bad). He said that he felt partially paralyzed (perhaps he had a mild case of botulism?). Before direction, they zigzag in as they approach closer and closer, the arc ever decreasing, until, when they are within a meter or two, they suddenly fold up their wings and drop straight down to the ground, whereupon they begin scurrying around frantically looking for the pile of warm, fresh dung that has attracted them from afar. Before you can even finish wiping yourself, beetles have already formed your dung up into balls and begun rolling it away! The largest species roll off large balls, the smaller ones take away smaller balls. The dung beetles fight over the balls of dung, sometimes taking it away from another beetle. They lay their eggs on these balls and bury them, their larvae later thriving on the nutrient-rich feces. Indeed, aside from disposing of toilet paper, one really need not bury crap in the Kalahari, for the dung beetles do it for you. As I indicated earlier, dung beetles have now been introduced into parts of Australia (unfortunately, not yet in the Great Victoria Desert) in an effort to reduce the food supply for bush flies!

The presence of so many big ungulates has an unfortunate consequence: Nasty, large blood-sucking ticks lurk wherever there is shade, awaiting a blood meal from a warm mammal. At first, we naïvely tried to rush into the shade, quickly throw down a cot, lie down on it, and check ourselves for ticks before taking our midday siestas. But, soon after, you were always awakened by the feeling of ticks crawling around on you looking for a nice soft place to bite (thank natural selection for body hair!). I am convinced that Kalahari ticks rain out of trees, dropping down on you. Due to this severe tick problem, we eventually gave up on exploiting natural shade and made our own tick-free shade well away from the shade of trees, using a tarp attached to the vehicle and propped up with tent stakes. As troublesome as these ticks were, I prefer them to Australian bush flies any day!

A very vocal gecko called the barking gecko (*Ptenopus garrulus*) chirps at dusk in the Kalahari, chorusing like frogs. These little lizards were difficult to collect because they seldom stray very far from their burrows. Ray Huey perfected his own "shovel trick" to catch *Ptenopus*. To attract females, males sing from the mouths of their burrows with just their head and foreparts out. If you approach slowly and silently, they will often hold their ground at this relatively safe spot. When you get within a couple of meters, you hold your shovel out at arm's length, and lunge suddenly, cutting off their retreat down their retiring for the night, we poured some water into the pot but never got around to cleaning up the dishes.

On this memorable night, after Larry and I went geckoing with the usual trepidation, the three of us (all big men) retired to sleep inside Molly (our Land Rover), one in the front seat and two abreast on top of our load in the rear. It was a hot summer night and unpleasant sleeping in such close quarters with all the rolling over, sweaty smells, and flatulence, but we had no real alternative, for there were hyaenas, leopards, and lions in the area. Hyaenas have enormous crushing jaws, and if you sleep out, when they come sniffing into camp they can chomp down on your head (natives have died this way, and survivors have facial scars to prove it). In the light of the moon after midnight, I awoke hearing a gurgling and slurping. I was very thirsty and said, "Hey, leave some for me. Pass the canteen when you're finished." There was no response whatsoever, as both my companions were still in deep slumber. Awakening more fully, I soon realized that the gurgling noise was coming from just outside the Land Rover. I peered out to see, silhouetted in the moonlight right outside the Land Rover, a huge hyaena—nearly the size of a Great Dane—slurping the water we had left soaking in our curry pot! When I woke Ray, his first instinct was to chase the hyaena away from the "off" stew. But then we realized, hey, it's a hyaena—they can eat *anything!* Certainly, a hyaena could handle that stew even if Ray couldn't.

One of my very fondest memories of the Kalahari is that of leaning against the hood of a trusty Land Rover ("Brunhilda") at sunset, sipping a Lion lager beer with two close friends and hearing the guttural roar of a wild black-maned Kalahari lion in the distance—my heartbeat picked up, and the hackles on the back of my neck stood up on end! Africa is certainly not a benign place like Australia!

Relieving oneself in the Kalahari is hazardous because of the predators, but quite an interesting adventure nevertheless, not nearly as unpleasant as it can be in Australia. Because of the presence of so many large ungulates, large numbers of dung beetles of several different species are exceedingly plentiful in the Kalahari. Before you have even finished depositing your load, you can hear them coming in for it, *bzzzzz, BZZZ, BZ,* thump! Small, medium-sized, and large dung beetles come in from downwind, homing in on the rich aroma of fresh fecal material with impressive precision. Swinging in great arcs from side to side until they lose the scent, then reversing

Barking gecko crucified by a shrike (still alive!)

burrow. Occasionally, you chop a gecko in half, but more often than not this technique worked well.

On a night when termites were swarming and sending out their winged reproductive alates, we found dozens of *Ptenopus* out well away from their burrows, feeding on the juicy soft-bodied termites. Some geckos were so stuffed that they could scarcely move, with their bellies full, their esophagi and their buccal cavities stuffed with termites hanging out of their mouths! Such gluttony has its risks. One unusual overcast day, when winged termites were swarming and going on mating flights during daylight hours, *Ptenopus*, normally strictly nocturnal, were actually active in daytime. Several species of shrikes (small predatory birds) were capturing these geckos and saving them for future meals by pinning them up on thorny *Acacia* bushes as food caches. There were dozens of crucified *Ptenopus*, many still alive, pinned up like Christmas tree ornaments festooning nearly every thorny bush in that part of the Kalahari that day.

Using eyeshine to collect geckos in the Kalahari, we found a beautiful semi-arboreal gecko, *Pachydactylus rugosus*, that had previously been thought to be rare. The favored microhabitat of this species was to perch about half a meter to a meter above ground on branches of the "wait-a-while" thorny bush *Acacia mellifera* (these plants are protected by vast numbers of recurved, cat's-claw-like thorns that snag your clothing and skin). Extracting these geckos from the wait-a-while bushes proved to be even more difficult than locating them!

One night while geckoing in Botswana, I came upon an unfamiliar small black snake. Treating it with proper caution as if it were venomous, I carefully pinned its head to the ground with a stick and picked it up, holding it by the neck closely behind the head. I dropped it into my collecting live jar and screwed on the screened lid. When Ray Huey returned from geckoing he asked me what I'd gotten, and I said, "Just a little black snake," offering him my live jar. He looked inside and exclaimed, "A burrowing sand viper! Did you know that *Atractaspis* is the only snake that can inject its venom into you while you're holding it behind the head?" This was the only burrowing sand viper we ever encountered—tally up yet another close call for lucky old Eric, who lives dangerously!

One of life's amenities most missed in the desert is cool beer. We became obsessed with solving this problem. One solution was to put beer out on the bonnet of the Land Rover at night. It often gets fairly chilly in the desert at night due to the clear skies. Before sunrise, pile the cool beers into a sleeping bag and wrap them well to keep them insulated and cool. By midday, when it has gotten hot, they are still acceptably "cold" beers, indeed. In the heat of the Kalahari summer, we perfected and enjoyed what we called "not-hot beer," which we cooled down by evaporation. Each beer was first wetted by dipping it in water, then rolled in toilet paper or in an absorbent paper towel. These are then placed in a basin of water and kept in the shade underneath the vehicle. The absorbent paper acts as a wick: as water evaporates, more is drawn up from the pan below. This worked best under windy conditions. If allowed to cool overnight, kept wet and in the shade, the beer stayed palatably cool well into the next day.

A small red sand viper, *Bitis caudalis*, was forever taking us by surprise and startling us. These little snakes, somewhat reminiscent of small sidewinder rattlesnakes, lie buried in the sand with only the tops of their heads showing, waiting to ambush their prey (largely lizards). When startled, they suddenly emerged from the sand, hissing and thrashing wildly, lifting themselves right off the ground, invariably causing our hearts to skip a beat (I'm not afraid of snakes, but whenever one takes me by surprise, I still jump!). Puff adders, which are the size of western diamondback rattlesnakes and equally dangerous, were even more imposing.

Once, in Arizona, after I shot with a BB gun a small, gray arboreal lizard (*Urosaurus graciosus*) in a shadscale shrub, the lizard fell down into the bush. I bent over, parting the branches and vegetation, peering in looking for the dead lizard specimen. Subliminally, I noticed a pile of dead leaves at the base of the shrub and thought that the lizard might have fallen into them. Just as I was about to reach further into the bush to try to find and extract the lizard, my eyes focused on the pile of dead leaves, which suddenly became a large western diamondback rattlesnake (*Crotalus atrox*). The blotched pattern, known as disruptive coloration, breaks up an animal's outline and provides effective camouflage.

A large Kalahari agamid lizard, *Agama hispida*, is unusual among lizards in that it has two enlarged fang-like canine teeth, large enough to draw blood. During the breeding season, males are exceedingly colorful, with yellow heads, bright blue nape, and red shoulders. The locals warned us that these lizards were venomous, explaining that agamas do not make their own poison, but obtain venom by "milking" cobras. When questioned further, Afrikaners explained to us that these lizards were often seen with their heads inside a cobra's mouth, extracting cobra venom. Of course, an alternative explanation for such an observation is simply that cobras eat these agamids!

Two species of Kalahari lacertid lizards, *Pedioplanus lineo-ocellata* and *Meroles suborbitalis*, sit and wait for prey, whereas two other species, *Heliobolus lugubris* and *Eremias namaquensis*, forage widely for their food. It took three of us to record time budgets for the movement patterns of individual lizards: one person watched a lizard with binoculars, shouting "start," "stop," "two meters," etc. A second person held two stopwatches, one in each hand, one stopped and the other running, one to accumulate time spent in motion, the other to time stationary positions, clicking both watches at each "start" and "stop," and hollering out the times to the third person (me). When a lizard was really moving, data poured in so fast that I was hard pressed to write it all down. In contrast, the three of us sometimes felt extremely foolish wasting our time standing around for long intervals waiting for a "sit-and-wait" lizard to move (do something, do anything, but do something, just move!).

Foraging widely is energetically expensive, and judging from their relative stomach volumes, those species that engage in this mode of food gathering appear to capture more prey per unit time than do sit-and-wait species. Overall energy budgets of widely foraging species are greater than those of sit-and-wait species. As would be expected, sedentary foragers tend to encounter and eat fairly mobile prey, whereas more active widely foraging predators consume less active prey. Compared with sit-and-wait species, widely foraging lacertid species eat more termites (sedentary, spatially and temporally unpredictable, but clumped prey). Another gorgeous widely foraging lacertid, *Nucras tessellata*, specializes on scorpions (by day, these large arachnids are nonmobile and very patchily distributed prey items).

Another ramification of foraging mode in these Kalahari lizards concerns exposure to their own predators. Because of their more or less continual movements, widely foraging species tend to be more visible, and as a result, suffer higher predation rates. Widely foraging species fall prey to lizard predators that hunt by ambush, such as the horned sand viper *Bitis caudalis*, whereas sit-and-wait lizard species tend to be eaten by predators that forage widely, such as Secretary Birds. Thus "crossovers" in foraging mode occur between trophic levels. Widely foraging lizard species are also more streamlined and have longer tails than sit-and-wait species.

When a small black lacertid with a bright red tail first appeared at a study site in Botswana, we thought initially that it might be a new species, perhaps even an undescribed one. But over the course of a few months, as these tiny lizards grew, they "metamorphosed" into *Heliobolus lugubris*. Juvenile *lugubris* have evolved a defense against predators by mimicking noxious beetles. These defenseless small Kalahari lacertid lizards mimic certain carabid beetles that emit pungent acids, aldehydes, and other repulsive chemicals when disturbed. (The local Afrikaans vernacular name for these beetles is "oogpister," which translates euphemistically as "eye squirter.") Adult *H. lugubris* are pale red and buff in color, matching the Kalahari sands, whereas juveniles have pitch-black bodies with white spots, and a reddish tail. Adult lizards walk in a normal lizard gait, with their vertebral columns undulating from side to side, but juveniles walk stiff-legged, with their backs arched vertically and their tails held flat against the ground as if they are trying to wipe their cloaca (presumably, this posture and the red color make their tails difficult to detect on the red Kalahari sands). When pursued, young *H. lugubris* abandon their "beetle walk" and dart rapidly for cover, using normal lizard locomotion. As they reach a snout-vent length of about forty-five to fifty millimeters (about the size of the largest oogpister beetles), these lizards metamorphose into the cryptic adult coloration and permanently abandon the arched walk. Once, when collecting oogpister beetles to measure their lengths, I actually stepped on and squashed a baby lizard, mistaking it for a beetle! Interestingly, the incidence of broken and regenerated tails is lower in juvenile *H. lugubris* than it is among other species of related lacertids in the same habitats, suggesting that this beetle mimicry may successfully reduce predatory attacks.

Five years later, in December 1975 and January 1976, under the auspices of a research grant from the National Geographic Society, I returned to the Kalahari with Ray Huey and professional photographer Carolyn Cavalier. We purchased a used white Land Rover pickup (christened Brunhilda), fitted the truck with a camper shell, filled her up with the requisite camping gear, and headed westward in the pouring rain toward the Kalahari-Gemsbok National Park (1975 was an exceedingly wet year). Upon arrival at the park, which was spectacularly green, we headed directly for one of our favorite study sites (Ludrille). We turned off the main park road at the unusually large *Acacia giraffe* tree that marked the spot, and headed

Pickling assembly line in the Kalahari (1970). Eric (right) weighs and measures each lizard while Ray Huey (center) records the data and Larry Coons (left) has the unenviable task of injecting each specimen with formaldehyde. (Tasks were rotated among the three of us from day to day.)

out across the usually dry watercourse of the Nossob River. Caught off guard by standing water and deep mud, Brunhilda was soon bogged! Moreover, there were two male lions under the tree only a few hundred meters away. Knowing full well how quickly a lion can run a hundred meters, with some trepidation Ray and I began to work to extract the vehicle from the mire. With Carolyn perched on top of Brunhilda with binoculars acting as our scout, Ray and I first unloaded the heaviest gear and then dug trenches to drain the water away from the wheels. When we were both a good distance away from Brunhilda, Carolyn suddenly let out a shriek! Instantly, both Ray and I looked toward the lion tree with sinking hearts (how fast could we run through that quicksand back to the safety of Brunhilda?). False alarm! Carolyn's exclamation was for her first sighting of wild Ostrich. After we got the Land Rover out of the mud, we drove over to the tree and found the two lions were on a kill—a young wildebeest (blue gnu). Hence, we had not been in any real danger because the lions were satiated.

Returning to a remote study site south of Tsabong, Botswana, we were distraught to find that the area had been burned and was being heavily grazed by cattle. Five years before it had been semipristine Kalahari desert wilderness, with fifteen species of lizards and spotted hyaena! When we drove in to the small village of Tsabong to get our passports stamped, we were greeted by a Canadian Peace Corps volunteer, who proudly announced that he and several others had spent the past several years helping the natives find bore water and establish cattle ranching over southern Botswana.

On both visits to the Kalahari, first in 1969–1970 and then again in 1975–1976, we made side trips to the Namib Desert, an ancient, exceedingly arid desert with a phenomenal diversity of beetles. Rain is almost nonexistent there, and most plants and animals live on the mist dropped by heavy oceanic ground fogs. Founded by the beetle expert Dr. Charles Koch, the Namib Desert Research Institute at Gobabeb lies on the Kuiseb river channel (usually dry), which flows from east to west, emptying into the South Atlantic near Walvis Bay. South of the Kuiseb lies the sand sea, with impressive windblown dunes reminiscent of those in the Sahara (the deBeer diamond fields are within this region). To the north of the riverbed are stony desert flats interrupted with granitic outcrops known as "koppes" (the Afrikaans equivalent of "tor"). At a magnificent site called the Spitzkoppe, we actually found San (Bushman) cave paintings, some depicting large game long since extinct in the area.

Later, in the coastal sand dunes, on a bitterly cold night when we were shivering inside our leather jackets, we were surprised and elated to find bizarre web-footed geckos (*Palmatogecko rangeri*). We also found the gecko *Ptenopus kochi*, which has enlarged toe lamellae ("fringed toes"). Both of these distinctive features presumably serve as "snowshoes" on the soft sands. Diurnal Namib lizards were equally fascinating. Flattened, diurnal, gray *Rhoptropus* geckos darted over rock outcrops, taking refuge in tight crevices under exfoliating slabs of granite. Shovel-nosed, fringe-toed lacertids (*Aporosaura anchieteae*) pulled a disappearing act by diving into the sand and "swimming" out of sight in sand dunes. Fringed toes have evolved independently in five different lineages of lizards (agamids, geckos, iguanians, lacertids, and skinks), constituting a beautiful example of convergent evolution in response to similar selective pressures.

Once we stopped for fuel at Rehoboth, not realizing that this was a city of half-castes, alienated from both white and black societies.

Needless to say, we were not given a very friendly reception. I also recall receiving some hateful, ugly looks from disenchanted, disenfranchised blacks. Another time, after a long drive, we pulled into a service station, primarily to relieve ourselves—I was floating, and had to empty my bladder urgently. But someone was in the "Blanke" toilet. In desperation, I went into the toilet designated for blacks—I was surprised and shocked to find no toilet or toilet paper, but only an open four-inch sewer drain, splattered with smelly feces and urine, which I peed down with great relief.

It is extremely fortunate that we undertook our Kalahari research when we did, before the worldwide outcry in protest against the Afrikaner policy of apartheid. Many people suffer under the illusion that the blacks in southern Africa are descendants of the original inhabitants. They are not. Before white settlement in the sixteenth century, southern Africa was populated entirely by the Khoi and Khoi-San people, small, light-skinned Bushmen. As the Afrikaners prevailed and built up prosperous farms in the wilderness, blacks ("Bantu") migrated in from the north and became workers for physical labor. San (Bushmen) were hunted down like animals and virtually exterminated, by both the emerging Afrikaners and the Bantu. (The predicament is thus rather more like our own American Indian/ex-African slaves situation.) Today, the standard of living is so much higher in South Africa that blacks infiltrate across the borders looking for work, much like illegal Mexican aliens do in the United States. Even in 1970, Namibia (then South West Africa) was "off limits" for research, and maps and weather records were "classified" information. Also, modern paved highways began at the border with South Africa, and there was a large, heavy concrete airport at the remote small city of Upington (both presumably for military reasons such as the war in Angola).

Several times during the past decade, I have received a chain letter from other well-meaning scientists, asking me to support a boycott against scientific research in South Africa. The letter requested that the international scientific community refuse to undertake or publish any research emanating from South Africa, and asked that all recipients write to the South African government decrying apartheid, and send the letter on to several other scientists with a moral conscience. We all must reach our own conclusions about such issues of human rights. If I had responded to this letter, I might well have jeopardized future research in South Africa. I feel strongly that scientists cannot allow politicians to cut off parts of the planet from scientific understanding. We must be allowed to make intercontinental comparisons. The entire planet is our domain and our laboratory, and we must be given access to it.

NOTE TO CHAPTER 10

1. Indeed, it is actually hazardous to walk under a weaver nest colony because a feeding cobra can fall trying to get into the downward-facing nest openings!

EVENTS AND AFTERTHOUGHTS

· · · · ·

AFTER WRITING MOST OF THIS BOOK, LATE IN 1992 I finally managed to acquire research grants from NASA and NSF to undertake a proper landscape ecology study of fires as an agent of disturbance using satellite imagery. To get these grants, it was essential to collaborate with experts in remote sensing: mechanical engineers. Two of these people, an endowed professor of mechanical engineering and a research engineer, came down under in July–August of 1992 (late wintertime in the Southern Hemisphere) to experience the outback first hand, and to acquire "ground truth" using the global positioning system (GPS), which receives signals from military satellites to estimate precise coordinates on the ground.

The engineers rented a four-wheel-drive Toyota flatbed pickup truck and camping equipment in Perth, and drove out, bringing along all the newest impressive high-tech GPS gear (this included two portable GPS receivers as well as a laptop computer). A rendezvous with my assistant Magnus and me was arranged at Red Sands (we had arrived a week before and were replacing drift fence and setting new pit traps). One receiver was established at the Red Sands Base Camp, the other was mobile, either hand-carried or taken in the truck. The differences between their two receptions from up to four satellites allowed calculation of exact locations on Earth.

My engineering colleagues elected to take a trip deeper into the desert to the Lake Yeo Nature Reserve to acquire data. Red Sands is on a pastoral lease called Yamarna, the most remote of all such leases,

OPPOSITE:
Karen and Gretchen climb a coastal sand dune near Eucla.

unprofitable, and one that will in all probability eventually be discontinued as a pastoral lease (both the Aborigines and C.A.L.M. are contenders for its stewardship). There had been a lot of rain, and I was concerned about getting bogged. We went out on what was intended to be a day trip in two four-wheel-drive vehicles, my assistant and I in Katy, the engineers in their rented Toyota pickup truck with their sleeping bags, "just in case something went wrong." To the east of Yamarna Homestead, tracks are totally unmaintained and really deteriorate quickly. The track is washed out in many places, with many potential bogs and sand traps (deep, loose, soft sand washed into the track by rains). At one point, a large marble gum had fallen across Len Beadell's track, blocking the road. Enterprising bushwhackers simply drove offroad around it until there was a sort of U hairpin curve in the track.

Though the track was rough, we reached Lake Yeo Reserve without incident and went some distance into it, had lunch, and decided to return to our base camp at Red Sands. As we departed, I said to the engineers, "If you don't make it back, we'll come looking for you tomorrow." They did not return. We were glad they had their sleeping bags, for it was a chilly night. The next day, we waited for them for a few hours, but when they failed to appear, we set out to look for them. Knowing that they might have had vehicle failure, I stopped by Yamarna Homestead and asked to borrow a tow chain, just in case they were broken down and we couldn't get the vehicle going. The station owner, Tom McCudden, gladly loaned us a chain, saying that he was pleased we were going out to get them (the job usually fell on him to rescue people in trouble in that remote part of the world).

Magnus and I discussed the possibilities: they might have merely had a flat tire and been unable to change it, or perhaps they did manage to get bogged, or perhaps they could have taken a corner too fast and rolled over. About twenty kilometers from Yamarna we came upon the research engineer walking back down the track for help. He said that they had stopped to take a picture of the fallen marble gum blocking the track, and that the truck wouldn't start up afterward. He indicated that there was some sort of an electrical failure, perhaps a dead battery? Then he mentioned that there was also a mysterious loose wire that didn't seem to go anywhere. We discussed the possibility of having to tow them over 30–40 km of rough road, and I asserted that we would only do that as an absolute last resort, that I had confidence that I could get their vehicle running and that they could drive it out. Even if their battery was dead, we could use my jumper cables to get their truck started.

Arriving at the scene, we found that they had built a bonfire and burned up about half the fallen gum tree. They said that they had spent a fairly miserable night, but they seemed in fairly good spirits and joked about sending the Main Roads Department a bill for clearing the roadblock. I took one look at the loose wire and noted immediately that it led to the car's electrical center. When I touched it to the positive battery terminal, I heard a relay click inside the electrical box (because they had left something on). I unscrewed the thumb screw on top of the terminal, inserted the end of the wire under it, tightened the thumb screw down, and told the research engineer to start the truck. He fussed around first, apparently in disbelief, testing first the windshield wipers and then the lights, but eventually tried to start the engine, which fired right up. In less than five minutes, we were escorting them back.

Returning the unused tow chain to Tom McCudden, I explained the relatively trivial problem they had and how easy it was to repair it. As we were spinning a yarn or two, the remote sensing engineers drove up. I said to McCudden, "Here come my engineers now," to which he responded, " . . . in theory only." This story underscores the necessity of knowing basic auto mechanics if one is planning to go bush.

My Australian mentor, A. R. "Bert" Main, told me the following tale. He was in the arid zone showing several visiting American biologists some of the biological treasures of arid Australia. In a dry lake bed, he noticed telltale traces that a frog had dug in to wait, torpid, for the next rains to fall. Bert announced to the Yanks that there was a frog a meter down right there, pointing to a very dry, and highly unlikely, spot. The Americans didn't believe him and proceeded to bet him a case of beer that there was no frog there. A day of hard digging ensued, when Bert finally won his hard-earned case of beer: standing in a pit up to his waist, he unearthed the torpid frog encased in its mucal sheath.

Sitting quietly in the fly-proof sanctity of my van, passing the heat of midday reading, I thought I heard the crack of a gunshot in the distance. Soon afterward I heard an engine, and then looked up to see an old Land Rover chugging cross-country toward my campsite, which was out of sight and a good kilometer off the main track. I got out and went to greet my uninvited visitors, still wearing my lizard "shotgun" revolver (recall that only law enforcement officers are allowed handguns down under). I was rather hirsute, as my beard and hair had been growing for more than a year. With my long gray beard, I must have looked a bit like a modern-day Moses. Their vehicle rolled to a stop as I sauntered up. It was two blokes out shooting rabbits and roos, the one in the passenger seat holding a rifle. The driver asked, "What're you doing out here?" to which I responded, "What are you doing? Just nosing around following other people's tracks?" He assured me that he hadn't been following my tracks at all, but that they had just been driving cross-country looking for something to shoot at when they saw my van in the distance and came over to investigate. When I told them that I'd been studying lizards here for the last twenty-five years, the rifleman said, "That's a long time," as if he thought that I'd been camped right there for a quarter of a century, like a Rip Van Winkle. He began to fidget, and they both became somewhat edgy, acting as if I must be some kind of a nut, perhaps dangerous, and they were eager to depart. I was glad to see them go—good riddance.

After a long, cold night, early one crisp winter morning at Red Sands, I took a roll of toilet paper and my shovel and climbed up a large sandridge to take my usual morning constitutional. As I came over the crest of the ridge, I was confronted by a large steaming mass of green. I didn't recognize it at first. Taken aback, I thought, What's this? It looked somewhat like a pile of viscera. Then it hit me, it was a huge pile of camel dung! And just dropped, too, since it was still warm ... looking more closely, I saw the telltale enormous plate-sized footprints of the great beasts. Only then did I look up and around: two enormous camels were standing a hundred meters away scrutinizing me intently, wondering what I was and who was invading their domain. Just when I felt that I was all alone, I had company, tons of big company! Moreover, they were engaged in exactly the same activity that I was.

Sometimes absolutes come into conflict, such as when the wind is blowing uphill. As every good camper knows, never pee into the wind. Likewise, never pee uphill. But what do you do when you have to go, and a strong wind is blowing uphill? Pee sideways? First, decide which "never" to violate. After some consideration, I elected to pee uphill, planning to watch for the inevitable rivulets, and to dance to sidestep them. I knew that it would be sheer folly to try to pee into the strong wind, for urine would certainly splatter all over my pants! But, surprisingly, my urine soaked immediately into the dry sand. So, in the desert at least, one can pee uphill, after all!

One of the more unpleasant things that can happen to you when you're living in the desert is to get what I call an "unquenchable thirst." You remain thirsty even after drinking all that you can hold. Water sloshes and gurgles in your belly, but you still are driven to drink more. I suspect this happens when body fluids fall to precariously low levels. In such a berserk state, I once drove hundreds of kilometers just to get to a place where I could get an iced drink!

The Coriolis force is reversed in the Southern Hemisphere: moving objects veer to the left instead of to the right, and water is reputed to go down drains counterclockwise instead of clockwise (this is much harder to demonstrate than it might seem). I sometimes idly muse about what these reversed forces might do to biological systems, composed as they are of dextro and levo isomeres of various carbohydrates, amino acids, and other organic molecules. Wouldn't it be bizarre if time spent in the opposite hemisphere had a rejuvenating effect! If so, my four years down under could lengthen my lifespan by eight years. But this argument is clearly specious. Breathing cleaner air, and drinking purer water might allow one to reduce bodily toxins, however.

Early on in my fieldwork, I managed to live out of the car. A military-style cot and a tarp sufficed to keep one off the ground and protected from the elements. Helen and I slept inside Matilda on top of our load. We went to great lengths to find ideal shady campsites, and we spent many an hour in the front seat, weighing and measuring lizards. When Karen and Gretchen came down, I rented a small house trailer fitted out to sleep four people, with closets, a kitchen table, its own built-in twenty-gallon water tank, a sink with a hand-pump faucet, a gas stove, and best of all, a propane refrigerator! This van also had a "tropical roof," an extra second roof about fifteen centimeters above the first roof, which kept it from getting so hot in the desert sun. By parking the van carefully, one could also enjoy shade at the critical times of day.

The luxury of having cold drinks plus the fly-proof sanctity offered by this van spoiled me so much that I purchased a similar old van of my own for the 1989–1991 season. I lived in this van for the better part of two years. Roads are very rough, often corrugated, in outback Australia, and they quickly tear up a trailer. Several leaf springs on this van broke, and I had difficulty obtaining adequate replacements. I made emergency repairs on the refrigerator after it rattled and broke loose from its moorings, but—alas—finally its cooling system sprang a leak, and it lost its refrigerant. Nearing the end of my second field season in March of 1991, I was heading out for one last trip to my remote desert study sites in Katy, towing the van behind, heavily loaded with food, water, and beer. Moving along about 45–50 km/hr, Katy and I hit a patch of brutal corrugations and suddenly ground to a stop. I got out to inspect things and noticed a flat tire on the van's right side, then walked around it and found that the left tire was also flat. I thought, "Damn, *two* flat tires!" Only then did I notice that both tires were splayed out at the bottoms and in at the tops—then I saw the great furrow gouged into the track by the van's snapped axle. I deliberated awhile before I decided that I had no real alternative but to abandon my creature comforts. Putting Katy into compound low four-wheel drive, I towed the trusty van off the track and out into the desert, leaving a deep grove behind. It was sad, and made me think of the song about the sinking of the Titanic. But, it was a fitting way to end my field season (if a few weeks premature).

Someday I would like to produce, direct, and perhaps even star in a movie entitled "Revenge of the Lizards," a sort of horror movie based on my own true story. The movie would begin with about an hour showing a dedicated field ecologist swatting bush flies and lizarding: noosing, grabbing, whomping, shooting, geckoing, digging, burning spinifex, running traplines, tracking, peering into burrows and hollows with mirrors, chopping lizards out of hollow logs, lighting dynamite fuses to smoke lizards out of hollows, and all the other assorted activities described above. You would see him taking cloacal temperatures; weighing, measuring, tagging, and preserving specimens; freezing tissues in liquid nitrogen; photographing; writing field notes; etc. Other scenes would show the intrepid scientist (and his assistants) back in the laboratory dissecting and measuring specimens, analyzing stomach contents, working with aerial photographs and satellite imagery to measure fire geometry, working up data on computers, writing papers, explaining and informing by giving cerebral lectures illustrated with elaborate graphs. Just about now, you are beginning to wonder why you came to see this boring movie.

Mid-movie the scene switches without warning. Suddenly, the star of the show is on trial for mass murder before a lizard judge and jury! The prosecution establishes that by his own records the defendant has single-handedly killed many thousands of innocent lizards. Maimed museum specimens are introduced as evidence that this has hardly been a euthanasia. Under direct examination, the scientist admits to planning and participating in the demise of many thousands of lizards. The defense attorney asks leading questions that help the ecologist to try to justify collecting all these lizards. He testifies that biologists must sacrifice some of their study organisms in order to gain understanding of them. He points out that his research has generated a textbook example of intercontinental comparisons. Most of his North American study sites are no longer desert, but have since been developed—if he hadn't collected the lizards when he did, there would be no record of what was once present there. Why aren't the developers that destroy desert habitats being tried? As to his collecting in Australia, he points out that his efforts have helped to discover previously unknown new species as well as to clarify phylogenetic relationships. His collections have been useful material for dozens of other scientists, who have used them in a variety of other kinds of studies, ranging from functional anatomy to systematics. The large series from particular study sites are valuable because they allow the appraisal of local populational variability within species. He also notes that the Australian deserts cover virtually millions upon millions of square kilometers, and that his study sites are merely a few tiny spots on this massive landscape. Further, he points out that even on sites that he has studied extensively, at the end of his study there are always just as many lizards and lizard tracks as there were at the outset. Finally, he argues that his collecting activities constitute about as much predation pressure as one pair of kestrels or a family of foxes. (Now there's a real criminal, the person who introduced European foxes into Australia!)

But the prosecution's emotional counterattack is devastating and vicious, claiming that all this killing was unnecessary, excessive, wanton, and merciless. In his summing-up arguments, the defense attorney tells the court that the scientist is in love with the deserts so much that he would lay down his own life to preserve them. The attorney says that the biologist would stop his research at once if he thought that his work in any way would allow the "greening" of the deserts. The lizard jury does not need to deliberate long before returning its verdict of guilty: the scientist has clearly committed mass murder. As the lizard judge readies to pronounce sentence— surely death by execution as for Nazi war criminals—our hero awakes, sweating profusely. Phew, it was only a nightmare . . . Back to real life.

Then comes the terrifying finale: once again the scientist is back in the Great Victoria Desert, collecting lizards. But this time, the Australian desert proves not to be quite so benign, after all. One day the lizard ecologist walks over the crest of a large sandridge and comes upon the track of a gigantic varanid, *Megalania prisca*. Its footprints are larger than human hands, and its stride measures nearly two meters. By extrapolation from perenties, our hero estimates that this giant varanid must be on the order of seven to eight meters long, larger than a good-sized man-eating crocodile. Excitedly, not even pausing to think to fear for his life, he decides that he must get a photograph of this great beast, which everyone knows has been extinct for millennia, to prove to the world that *Megalania* still roams the Australian interior. As he sets out bravely with his camera and telephoto lens, the hunter becomes the hunted. He first realizes this when the lizard tracks he is following begin to follow his own! Only then, looking behind himself for the first time, does he realize that an enormous *Megalania* is stalking him like a cat stalks a mouse! After snapping a few quick photos, he makes a sudden break for the safety of the car, running with a marked limp as fast as he can! But alas, it's no use, the great beast pursues, closes quickly, pounces on and captures him, and devours him alive! Trick photography with real perenties made to look four to five times their actual size would be exceedingly realistic and effective. Add in a wife and daughters, pretty females, stretch out the terror scenes a little, and you have all the elements for a truly spectacular terrestrial equivalent of *Jaws*.

References

ALLAN, G. E., AND G. F. GRIFFIN.
1986   Fire ecology of the hummock grasslands of central Australia. In
        Proc. 4th Biennial Conference of the Australian Rangeland Society,
        126–129. Armidale, Australia, August 24–27.

BAGLIN, D., AND B. MULLINS.
1969   *Captain Cook's Australia*. Sydney: Horowitz Publications.

BURBIDGE, A. A., K. A. JOHNSON, P. J. FULLER,
AND R. I. SOUTHGATE.
1988   Aboriginal knowledge of the mammals of the central deserts of
        Australia. *Australian Wildlife Research* 15:149–156.

BURBIDGE, N. T.
1943   Ecological succession observed during regeneration of Triodia
        pungens R. Br. after burning. *Journal of the Royal Society of
        Western Australia* 28:149–156.

BURROWS, N., B. WARD, AND A. ROBINSON.
1991   Fire behaviour in spinifex fuels on the Gibson Desert Nature
        Reserve, Western Australia. *Journal of Arid Environments*
        20:189–204.

ESTES, R.
1983   The fossil record and early distribution of lizards. In *Advances
        in Herpetology and Evolutionary Biology*, ed. A. G. J. Rhodin and
        K. Miyata, 365–398. Cambridge, Mass.: Museum of Compara-
        tive Zoology.

FINLAYSON, H. H.
1943   *The Red Centre*. Sydney: Angus and Robertson.

GREER, A. E.
1989   The biology and evolution of Australian lizards. Surrey Beatty
        & Sons Pty. Limited.

GRIFFIN, G. F., N. F. PRICE, AND H. F. PORTLOCK.
1983   Wildfires in the central Australian rangelands 1970–1980.
        Journal of Environmental Management 17:311–323.

HUEY, R. B., AND E. R. PIANKA.
1977   Natural selection for juvenile lizards mimicking noxious
        beetles. *Science* 195:201–203.

HUEY, R. B., AND E. R. PIANKA.
1977   Seasonal variation in thermoregulatory behavior and body
        temperature of diurnal Kalahari lizards. *Ecology* 58:1066–1075.
        (With an appendix by J. A. Hoffman.)

HUEY, R. B., AND M. SLATKIN.
1976   Costs and benefits of lizard thermoregulation. *Quarterly Review
        of Biology* 51:363–384.

MINNICH, R. A.
1983   Fire mosaics in southern California and northern Baja Califor-
        nia. *Science* 219:1287–1294.

MOLNAR, R. E.
1985   The history of lepidosaurs in Australia. In *Biology of Australasian
        Frogs and Reptiles*, ed. G. Grigg, R. Shine, and H. Ehmann,
        155–158. Chipping Norton, N.S.W.: Surrey Beatty & Sons Pty
        Limited.

MORTON, S. R., AND C. D. JAMES.
1988   The diversity and abundance of lizards in arid Australia: A new
        hypothesis. *American Naturalist* 132:237–256.

PEFAUR, J. E., AND W. E. DUELLMAN.
1980   Community structure in high Andean herpetofaunas. *Trans.
        Kansas Academy of Science* 83:45–65.

PIANKA, E. R.
1966   Convexity, desert lizards, and spatial heterogeneity. *Ecology*
        47:1055–1059.

PIANKA, E. R.
1967   On lizard species diversity: North American flatland deserts.
        Ecology 48:333–351.

PIANKA, E. R.

1968   Notes on the biology of *Varanus eremius*. *Western Australian Naturalist* 11:39–44.

PIANKA, E. R.

1969   Notes on the biology of *Varanus caudolineatus and Varanus gilleni*. *Western Australian Naturalist* 11:76–82.

PIANKA, E. R.

1969   Habitat specificity, speciation, and species density in Australian desert lizards. *Ecology* 50:498–502.

PIANKA, E. R.

1969   Sympatry of desert lizards (*Ctenotus*) in Western Australia. *Ecology* 50:1012–1030.

PIANKA, E. R.

1973   The structure of lizard communities. *Annual Review of Ecology and Systematics* 4:53–74.

PIANKA, E. R.

1975   Niche relations of desert lizards. Chapter 12 in *Ecology and Evolution of Communities*, ed. M. Cody and J. Diamond, 292–314. Cambridge: Harvard University Press.

PIANKA, E. R.

1985   Some intercontinental comparisons of desert lizards. *National Geographic Research* 1:490–504.

PIANKA, E. R.

1986   *Ecology and Natural History of Desert Lizards: Analyses of the Ecological Niche and Community Structure*. Princeton: Princeton University Press.

PIANKA, E. R.

1989   Desert lizard diversity: Additional comments and some data. *American Naturalist* 134:344–364.

PIANKA, E. R.

1992   A land of lizards. *Landscope* 7 (3):10–16.

PIANKA, E. R.

1992   Fire Ecology. Disturbance, spatial heterogeneity, and biotic diversity: Fire succession in arid Australia. *Research and Exploration* 8:352–371.

PIANKA, E. R.

1993   The many dimensions of a lizard's ecological niche. Chapter 9 in *Lacertids of the Mediterranean Region*, eds. E. D. Valakos. W. Böhme, V. Perez-Mellado, and P. Maragou, 121–154. Hellenic Zoological Society, University of Athens, Greece.

PIANKA, H. D., AND E. R. PIANKA.

1970   Bird censuses from desert localities in Western Australia. *Emu* 70:17–22.

PULLIAM, H. R.

1988   Sources, sinks, and population regulation. *American Naturalist* 132:652–661.

PYNE, S. J.

1991   *Burning Bush: A Fire History of Australia.* New York: H. Holt & Co., Inc.

RALPH, W.

1984   Fire in the centre. *Ecos: C.S.I.R.O. Environmental Research* 40:3–10.

RECHER, H. F.

1981   Fire and the evolution of the Australian biota. Chapter 7 in *Ecological Biogeography in Australia*, ed. A. Keast, 137–162. The Hague: W. Junk.

ROLSTON, H.

1985   Duties to endangered species. *BioScience* 35:718–726.

STORR, G. M.

1968   The genus *Ctenotus* (Lacertilia, Scincidae) in the eastern division of Western Australia. *Journal of the Royal Society of Western Australia* 51:97–109.

TAYLOR, F. B.

1910   Bearing of the Tertiary mountain belt on the origin of the earth's plan. *Bulletin Geological Society of America* 21:179–226.

VITT, L. J., AND J. D. CONGDON.

1978   Body shape, reproductive effort, and relative clutch mass in lizards: Resolution of a paradox. *American Naturalist* 112:595–608.

WINKWORTH, R. E.

1967   The composition of several arid spinifex grass-lands of central Australia in relation to rainfall, soil water relations, and nutrients. *Australian Journal of Botany* 15:107–130.

INDEX

This book is set in Janson Text.

Printed on 60 lb Finch Opaque
and bound by Edwards Brothers,
Ann Arbor, Michigan.

Color section and dust jacket
printed on 100 lb Consolith by
New England Book Components,
Hingham, Massachusetts.

Designed and composed by
Ellen McKie on a Macintosh
in PageMaker 5.0 for the
University of Texas Press.